# Black Women
# and the
# Peace Movement

# Black Women and the Peace Movement

## by Wilmette Brown

Foreword by Janice Owens

Introduction by Juliet Yelverton

FALLING WALL PRESS

Published by Falling Wall Press

First edition published by the International Women's Day Convention
August 1983
This edition published June 1984

Typeset by Falling Wall Press
Printed in Great Britain by Colourways Press Ltd., Clevedon
Bound by Paperback Binders, Abingdon


ISBN 0 905046 26 9




Falling Wall Press Ltd.
75 West Street, Old Market, Bristol BS2 0BX, England

# Contents

# Foreword
## to the First Edition

Let me declare my interest straight away — I am a very average middle-aged white woman. But I have three Black daughters, and a vested interest in the kind of world they have to live in.

When a lot of money is spent on my behalf by the government, when laws are passed for me by elected representatives, I am told that this is necessary for defence, for security. Well, all those nuclear warheads don't defend my daughters against the insults offered to Black people in a racist society. They don't offer much security to girls in a sexist society. And if they were actually used they wouldn't do much for the people of any nation, not even the government of any nation.

What a silly idea it is anyway, this 'nation' that has to have a Defence of the Realm Act, and a Nationality Act and the Official Secrets Act, so that we can enjoy life in a 'free market economy'. I watch the programmes on TV sometimes, and wonder who they're really for, especially the advertisements. Sometimes I listen to 'Today in Parliament' and feel that I am totally omitted, left out, non-existent: very few voices speak for me when the debates are droning on, even when really important aspects of my life are the subject.

Black people must feel that more often, and more strongly. If I don't accept that Margaret Thatcher speaks for me when she refers to the need to 'preserve the fabric of our daily life', my daughters must find her speeches even less relevant. They might even feel a quick flood of fear, which has to be pushed down, hidden from strangers, left to tie knots in the gut.

So I have an interest in searching for Peace, and I

share that interest with Wilmette Brown. We have worked together in the Peace Working Group of the Greater London Council's Women's Committee since the first meeting in December 1982, and as part of the group of women organising the 8 March 1983 International Women's Day Convention on 'Women and Peace' at County Hall. At the Convention, Wilmette first presented her paper on *Black Women and the Peace Movement*, which sparked an enthusiastic discussion.

Wilmette is right when she says, 'One of the biggest ripoffs of the peace movement has been to hide how it has always been Black and white.' Right now in England it can sometimes seem to be the preoccupation of propertied white women with career opportunities who are out to protect their own. But for white people there are problems of racism and elitism that are in no way secondary to the search for peace, and to work with feminists, or among groups of women who are not necessarily feminists, is a good starting-point for examining what sickness lies at the engine of the arms race. The connections exist, and we must find them. Or anyway, I must because I have these daughters, who are much too good to waste.

Janice Owens
*Convenor of the Peace Working Group*
*April 1983*

8

# Introduction
## to the First Edition

I first met Wilmette Brown at the English Collective of Prostitutes' 12-day Occupation of the Church of the Holy Cross in London in November 1982.* News of the Occupation came to me through a scribbled note from Arlene at Greenham. The general spirit of the note was 'Whores and lesbians take over church. At last things are moving!' I caught the spirit of her optimism, that the vulnerable were gathering strength and making a stand against the State. I came along to the church to give my support and gain support for myself. I don't feel confident about confronting authority, but I do feel sure that people of all kinds have got to combine our efforts in doing so. That way we will be stronger.

Since being at Greenham and Molesworth, I had been in touch with lesbian women, but not to my knowledge with whores. I was anxious to meet them, so came to the church Occupation prepared to do what I could. It was a good experience which we are both benefitting from. We are building links and our struggle gains strength.

The same kinds of consideration applied to the church Occupation as would be to a peace protest. Things such as media misrepresentation; police response – how to judge it; having our case taken seriously; anxiety about not being misled by sweet sounding but otherwise empty words – as the Labour Party has done to us in the past.

Before the Occupation, which was against police

* See my article in *Peace News*, 27 May 1983, pp. 12-13.

illegality and racism towards women in the King's Cross red-light area, I hadn't realized the depth of vulnerability that Black people, especially Black women, feel in regard to the police. But listening to Wilmette and the other women inside the church, I began to put my own feelings and experience with the police together with Black women's.

My feelings are based on a deep class suspicion which knows that the police as an institution aren't out to protect our interests or even seek to understand them — despite the fact that many police as individuals do not fit into my generalization. Unfortunately, such an institution corrupts the morality of its members.

I was arrested outside the US Embassy in London in June 1982, when six of us — five women and a man — staged a 'die-in' on the Embassy steps as part of a protest against President Reagan's visit to Britain during his tour of Europe during the Nato Special Session on Disarmament.

The procedure in such a situation is that the Embassy has to request the police to move us. They cannot arrest us since we are on 'foreign soil'. No such request was made from the Embassy. The police acted illegally, chased us up the steps and arrested us immediately without giving us the statutory warning. The police dragged or carried us off the steps and piled us on the pavement, standing over us until the police van came. In court they lied and said we had fallen on the pavement and they had arrested us for 'obstruction of the highway'.

I was placed in the gutter. I lay there, keeping my eyes closed. It was my first experience of such an action, and I had been advised that it was best to do this: 'Once dead, stay dead'. Two policemen stood over me, discussing our action and attempting to wind me up by making derogatory comments. When the police van came, one said to the other, 'Which end do you want to carry? The end that bites or the end that stinks?'

As we were piled on top of each other in the van, we had no chance to get up. Angela, who suffers badly from arthritis, attempted to sit up but was pushed down again. She was at the bottom of the pile with her back against the metal ridges along the floor. The police crowded into the van, one placing his leg across my throat. They drove off deliberately swerving, hitting curbs and braking hard to cause us as much discomfort as possible, amidst wisecracks of 'Bet you didn't pass your driving test that way', and 'We shouldn't have put the man with the women, you don't know what they might get up to. With this lot you can't put the women next to the women.'

Much of this is common behaviour with the police. In the words of one policeman at Greenham, 'When I put on my uniform, I'm no longer human.'

At recent peace demonstrations. police upon State directives have played it very cool. Not arresting, not wanting to draw public attention and condemnation in their treatment of a 'peaceful demonstration'. But if you look back to the 60s, you see that they have used water cannons on peace demonstrations in Britain, and even now with 'friendly policing', there are individual cases of malice. On 12 December at Greenham, one woman had her arm broken; another was very roughed up by the police, leaving her in a state of shock. There were also reports of nipple-twisting and pressure-pointing.

Of course, the media are keen to help the police present a good face. When I did an interview with Radio Cambridge, they edited it and said: 'We don't need to talk about police violence.'

In Italy, the police are a lot more openly fascist in their dealings with peace demonstrators. At recent women-only demonstrations at Comiso, the proposed cruise missile base in Sicily, several women had their arms broken and other Dutch and English women were deported under machine-gun supervision.

11

The greatest fear about the police in Britain lies in legislation which seeks to give them extra powers; and proposals that demonstrators should pay the cost of their own policing. Both are further incursions on our freedom in protesting against the State — forcing us ultimately into more direct confrontation.

The National Front movement also thrives in a State where such fascist measures are becoming general policy. At Christmas 1982 our peace camp in London was attacked, and one of our members seriously injured, by NF youths. They equated peacemakers with 'lefties' — a view which is frequently expressed by Tory politicians, another example of divisive politics and something which Greenham women have sought to counteract in their appeal to all women.

This summer a group of us are also hoping to draw allegiance across barriers and are also opening our minds to the struggle of other groups in 'A Walk for Life' from Faslane in Scotland to Greenham, from 19 May to 6 August, 1983. We're hoping that many different people will join us. Whilst I'm fully in support of women-only action at Greenham — women do need space to politicise — I feel that we also need to demonstrate our unity with men on issues which profoundly affect everyone. Likewise between Black and white people.

Juliet Yelverton
*Molesworth Peace Camp and 'A Walk for Life' organiser*
*April 1983*

# Preface
# to the Second Edition

*Black Women and the Peace Movement* was first published in August 1983. That edition soon ran out, and this second edition has been revised and expanded. It now includes the edited transcript of a speech in January 1984 at a Bristol meeting attended by 150 women and organised by a group of Black and white women. It was one of many meetings, involving Black and white women and men, which were organised to carry on the mushrooming discussion launched by the first edition.

The original essay gave a new general perspective on the peace movement. But the question remained: how does this work in practice? How does racism, which we are struggling to overcome in the peace movement as in the rest of the world, actually function to promote war; what exactly are we divided by and what can bring us together? The Bristol speech, 'Across the Divide of Race, Nation and Poverty: Women Organising for Peace', confronts these questions. Its aim is to help the explosive discussion which the first edition generated, to be more specific, more down to earth, to spring from people's actual experience within and outside the movement.

I hope that my catalogue of racism, separatism and careerism, and my description of the possibilities of Black and white women organising together in spite of these divides, will encourage other women, Black and white, to say what they know.

I want to thank Suzie Fleming for transcribing the Bristol speech, and for her queries on both texts, which spurred me on to try to explain myself more clearly.

13

Thanks also to Denise Green and Jeremy Mulford at Falling Wall Press for much forbearance with missed deadlines and changes during the typesetting.

I am grateful to Selma James for every aspect of producing this book: for editing with insight and patience, and for the rich dialogue this gave rise to; for her time and emotional housework at moments of crisis; for her analysis which laid the basis for the Wages for Housework Campaign; and for her tireless and inventive organising which confirms again and again the Campaign's premise, that Black and white women can see eye to eye. Thank you, Selma.

Thanks last but not least to the women of the King's Cross Women's Centre, and to Solveig Francis, joint co-ordinator of the Centre with me, for taking up the slack when my head was in these pages. Power to the sisters.

Wilmette Brown
18 May 1984
Bristol
Not another brick in the wall.

# Black Women and the Peace Movement

## widening the issue of peace

*. . . up to now many of us have been told to forget our own needs in some wider interest which was never wide enough to include us.*
Selma James[1]

At the first meeting of the Peace Working Group of the Greater London Council Women's Committee in December 1982, a woman from Greenham Common Women's Peace Camp asked me, as the only Black woman there, to talk about what the peace movement — so visibly white and middle class — could do to involve more Black people. To paraphrase her, it is particularly obvious in an international city like London, that to win, the peace movement must be seen also to be Black.

I think she spoke for the slowly and painstakingly growing numbers of white people who are grasping the importance of fighting racism against Black people — not as an act of charity or a favour to somebody else, but because it interferes with their own lives. But it is

15

still altogether too rare in the women's movement, or in the movement generally, for racial divisions to be discussed without either guilt-tripping white people, or blaming Black people, or both.

It testifies to the Greenham Common women's determination to win, and to what their struggle has already taught them, that it was the woman from Greenham who raised the issue of Black participation self-critically: that is, as a challenge to the peace movement to re-evaluate their organising and their priorities, and from the point of view of her responsibility to make dialogue possible between Black and white women. For me that was already a victory: another victory of Greenham Common.

But it's a hard row to hoe.

Several good things began to appear at that meeting: women informed the group about peace issues and initiatives in their different London boroughs; we worked out terms of reference for the group which took account of our discussion about Black people's situation internationally in relation to peace; and we made a start at working out how to put this awareness of the connections between race and peace into practice by getting a 'peace bus' that could go around to all kinds of different London neighbourhoods, relating the issue of peace to local communities' problems and needs.

We also debated the issue of women's autonomy in the peace movement: on the one hand, with the power behind us of the overwhelmingly successful women's demonstration at Greenham the week before, on 12 December, 1982;[2] and on the other, with an eye to the backlash from some men and women in the press the week after, against a women-only demonstration.

But a white woman who arrived late at the meeting was very upset at what I was saying about Black people and peace. She interrupted me as I was describing a man I had seen at Greenham on 12 December, wearing a badge that said 'Yanks go home!', as an example of how, like racism, nationalism can be divisive in the peace movement. I was making the point that there's a world of difference between people in the US and the US government; that as a Black American I do not want to be identified with Ronald Reagan's warmongering; and that the peace movement in the United States has taken on new life by taking leadership from women organising for peace in Europe.

She argued that we shouldn't 'widen the issue' away from peace; that we should be discussing what Europeans were going to do about peace. As far as she was concerned, challenging racism and nationalism was a diversion from 'peace'. But the 'European solution' she called for cannot escape confronting racism and nationalism, since Europeans are by no means uniform or united by nation or race.

The debate in the Peace Working Group over how wide to make the issue of peace is going on throughout the peace movement. It is in no way peculiar to that particular meeting – or even that particular movement. In the history of the Black movement in the United States, when Martin Luther King came out against the Vietnam War he had to answer 'those who ask the question, "Aren't you a civil-rights leader?" and thereby mean to exclude me from the movement for peace . . .'[3]

Black people in Europe, and since the 1980-82 urban rebellions, most visibly in Britain, are preoccupied in daily survival with 'wider' issues which are inseparable from peace. For example, three 'wider issues' that particularly preoccupy Black people in Britain are immigration, education and the police. What is becoming increasingly clear is how integral these three issues are to the peace movement.

While for Black people organising about immigration may focus on the Nationality Act – which threatens us with deportation and divides our families – the freedom of peace activists to cross international boundaries is also about immigration.[4] What is immigration about if not our freedom to make a life for ourselves — including organising to save our lives — wherever we choose?

While Black people are preoccupied with racism in education and the schools programming our children for menial jobs and low wages, peace organisers are concerned with the schools programming our children to be perpetrators and victims of war.[5] But low wages and scarce jobs are a necessary part of the climate of military buildup; and when people are unemployed they may have less power to resist being used as cannon fodder.[6] Young people in Britain, Black and white, women and men, are being made vulnerable to military recruitment by high teenage unemployment; and the Youth Training Scheme makes military training even more attractive.

As for the police, the Greenham Common women, like the Black movement, have begun to document police violence against them for stepping out of line.[7] The use of a massive police presence to prevent workers from picketing and from moving from one part of Britain to another to organize in the current miners' strike makes undeniably clear that the police are a domestic army but an army nonetheless. Police activity on a daily basis in Black communities, and whenever they deem necessary, against any group which moves 'out of place', clue us in that what governments really mean by deterrence is deterrence of social change; that the function of all State armies is to deter struggle for a new age at home and abroad.

# black women's autonomy

*I have done a great deal of work – as much as a man, but did not get so much pay. I used to work in the field and bind grain... but men never doing no more, got twice as much pay. So with the German women. They work in the field and do as much work, but do not get the pay. We do as much, we eat as much, we want as much. What we want is a little money. You men know that you get as much again as women . . . for what you do. When we get our rights, we shall not have to come to you for money, for then we shall have money enough of our own. You have been having our right so long, that you think, like a slaveholder, that you own us. I know that it is hard for one who has held the reins for so long to give up; it cuts like a knife. It will feel all better when it closes up again. When woman gets her rights man will be right. How beautiful that will be. Then it will be peace on earth and good will to men.*

Sojourner Truth, former slave, 1867[8]

Women do two-thirds of the world's work, get 5% of world income and own 1% of world assets.[9] Women's experience trying to change the world: whether as Black mothers defending our sons from 'sus',[10] police harassment, courts and jail; rape survivors defending ourselves; prostitutes or lesbians demanding civil rights; or peace organisers protesting Cruise and nuclear power, most bears out that the police – like the neutron bomb – are not there to protect us, but to protect property from the world's people who have produced it and especially from those who are the poorest. Yet Minister of Defence Michael Heseltine, who places people's lives in mortal danger every minute, accuses peace women of using violence to prevent him from speaking. It reminds me of the Establishment accusing Black people of

19

racism when we organise to protect ourselves from racism.

The military monopoly of world resources: the arms trade to prop up dictatorships; the pillage of raw materials from the Third World; the concentration of industrial and technological development on the war machine means that in Bangla Desh women spend several hours a day just fetching water; while in Harlem or the East End of London, older women annually die of cold or starve to death with Reagan and Thatcher cuts. Between North and South, and in the South which is within the North, the military-industrial complex daily turns Third World countries and inner city ghettoes into ecological disaster areas.[11] From the point of view of women of colour, who are the majority of the majority of the world's people, and also the poorest, the threat of nuclear war and nuclear power is inseparable from day-to-day military-industrial repression: 'sex', 'race' and 'class' issues are 'peace' issues.

But Black women's autonomy — the autonomy of those of us with the least power and therefore most in jeopardy — is the best protection for everyone that all the issues of survival — that is, all the issues of peace — will come out. In the civil rights, national liberation and Black Power movements of the 50s and 60s, Black people drove a wedge into the international Establishment that opened a way for the present women's movement, just as the movement for the abolition of Black slavery had opened a way for the women's movement of the 19th century. But where Black men are in charge of the Black movement, Black women's views are never fully taken into account; and so it is with white women in charge of the women's movement. Black women are still fighting for white women and Black and white men to acknowledge that the women's movement is both Black and white, and that the Black movement is women and children as well as men.

Just as women's autonomy in the peace movement, most visibly and powerfully exemplified at Greenham, has expanded what the whole movement is capable of — by expanding the capacity of the least powerful to speak for ourselves, Black women's experience raises survival issues for the whole of the Black community, for the whole of the Black movement and for the whole of the peace movement, from the bottom up. In this era of Margaret Thatcher; Indira Gandhi, whose government was once brought down by massive protests against forced sterilisation; and Eugenia Charles, prime minister of Dominica, who stood beside Ronald Reagan as he announced the invasion of Grenada, we should have no illusions that white or Black women being in charge guarantees justice; just as a long line of Black heads of State should by now have convinced us that substituting Black faces for white does not guarantee liberation. But the work of building the peace movement, and all the other movements, cannot be accomplished so long as Black women's contribution is hidden. Black women's situation and struggle at the bottom of the world hierarchy — with the most work and the least wealth — must set the terms, that is, be the reference point and yardstick for what to take into account, in working out how victory can belong to all of us.

These are some of the most basic terms. Since Black women are most vulnerable, more powerful sectors of the movement must work together with us on planning and implementing how we are to be protected — in order to protect the movement, in order to protect themselves. When the police move, we are their first targets. Afro-Americans used to say in the 60s that white radicals can always take a bath, cut their hair, and rejoin the mainstream. Our abiding fear, confirmed by experience, is that sooner or later we will be deserted on the firing line.

Cooped up and stranded in some of the most dank

and decrepit housing, in some of the most noisy and polluted areas, with the least access to public transport and social services, we need for more powerful sectors to understand that because we are poor doesn't mean we are stupid. When we are not visible in the peace movement it doesn't mean we are not fighting for peace. Like the majority of working class people, especially women, we are terribly overworked, terribly underpaid and often too exhausted to rally to any cause beyond immediate survival. What it means when we are not at peace demonstrations is that we have had to make other priorities for peace because we have so little time and money.

Besides, being Black women doesn't make us less fearful of confronting the State than the majority of white people who are also not on demonstrations. If there is such a thing, perhaps ours are the most understandable reasons to cop out. What can most prevent us from copping out, however, is visible support and acknowledgement of the peace movement's common cause with us on the issues where we are organising most visibly: we need mutual respect for our priorities, and recognition that although our areas of work in the movement are different, they are nevertheless mutually indispensable.

One of these areas of difference is over violence. And I am not talking about the self-destructive violence within and between sectors of the working class, of men towards women, of white people towards Black people, of adults towards children. As long as Black people are denied self-determination, reliable allies, and the resources to liberate ourselves, we are forced to resort to our power to destroy − as the only power we have, and as the only way to get more power. In that context our violence is always in self-defence, and white people who have more power than we do, counselling us against violence, place themselves in the indefensible position of presuming to choose our weapons for us — like men's presumption in complaining that women are shrill or aggressive — or violent. How we fight for our lives depends on what tools and supports are available to us; but we are determined to fight.

Black women's autonomy also means setting the same terms for ourselves as we set for other people. We have experienced enough careerism in the Black and women's movements to refuse to tolerate double standards among ourselves: among Black women, no less than among men or white women, our point of reference must be from the bottom up. One way of making a career off racism and/or sexism is by refusing to embrace other sectors who are in struggle. Exclusivity and separatism are attractive to prospective employers in the race and gender relations industries, because by helping to perpetuate the sex, race and class divisions among us, they perpetuate those industries. Isolating ourselves from other sectors also isolates the least powerful sectors of Black women from the help they need, help which more powerful sectors could provide. No Black woman can afford the luxury of either dismissing peace as a white issue, or allowing racism in the peace movement to go unchecked so that she has a convenient, even profitable — but self-destructive — excuse for not participating.

At the same time, connecting with other sectors in the peace movement can't mean giving up the areas where we are already organising. It is that work which enables Black people to contribute new resources, tactics, energies and understanding of what we're up against, what is at stake — in other words, more power and new directions — to the movement for peace. Nor does making connections within the peace movement mean abandoning the autonomy of Black women's groups or of Black community organisations we belong to already. On the contrary, Black women are already part of the peace movement, and the challenge of our autonomy is, on the one hand, to bring the power of our particular focus to other sectors of the movement and, on the other, to draw power from them for our particular focus. One essential meaning of autonomy is taking the responsibility to work out how best to accomplish this mutual exchange of power in our organising.

We educate more powerful sectors out of racism and sexism not by rhetoric, accusations and 'explanations', which can amount to a kind of game, but by doing the work of our own autonomous organising – which includes proposing to other sectors the kind of support we need them to give, as well as listening for and acknowledging their proposals, so that everyone's skills are integrated into the work of winning. On these terms we have no excuse not to work with people who have proved they are determined to pool resources with us and win.

We need the hard-won resources of the peace movement – people, information, connections, expertise – also to be put at the disposal of fighting the survival issues that appear most immediately to involve Black people, but really involve everybody. For example, the Nationality Act and internal passport controls terrorise Black people and immigrants into not demonstrating for peace; while the Police Bill threatens to drive underground everybody's organising, whether for peace or for any other issue. This is not an uneven trade: Black women, Black people as a whole, have built up quite a store of resources for struggle, which we have already turned over to peace movements past and present.

# black herstory

*No amount of gold could provide an adequate compensation for the exploitation and humiliation of the Negro in America down through the centuries. Not all the wealth of this affluent society could meet the bill. Yet a price can be placed on unpaid wages.*
Martin Luther King Jr.[12]

The biggest ripoffs of the peace movement have been to hide both how it has always been Black and white, and how women have always been the backbone. Beyond acknowledging Martin Luther King as a great man, for women to know our own herstory in the Black, the women's and the peace movements, we must look to the Black women who were behind him. Building on the power of an international movement, as women are doing today, King learned from Gandhi's experience of successful non-violent direct action in India. Today the movement of so-called 'Untouchables' in India, builds on the accomplishments of the Black movement in the US. One way that women of African and Asian descent can build practical unity among ourselves here in Britain is by exploring together the contributions of African and Asian women to these earlier peace movements.

Many people know that the visible phase of the civil rights movement, for which Martin Luther King eventually became the standard-bearer, was touched off in 1955 by the non-violent direct action of a Black woman named Rosa Parks, tired on her way home from work, who refused to move to the Black section at the back of the bus in Montgomery, Alabama. Fewer people know that Martin Luther King was assassinated while he was organising for the Poor People's Campaign, which was to culminate in a tent city of poor people of all colours on the lawns of State power in Washington DC. 1968: I have seen in a film documentary of those last few months of Martin Luther King's life that as he moved towards his most profound challenge to the US military-industrial complex, among his points of reference were the Black welfare mothers of Mississippi, the poorest of the old slaveholding states, who were refusing to send their sons to Vietnam to kill and die for a State which kept them on the edge of starvation.

Throughout the 60s, Black welfare mothers had organised a nationwide movement of non-violent direct action to raise the living standards of the poorest people in the richest nation on earth. They had won increased money and services for themselves, their children and men in the Black community. They had spread the wealth around by a campaign of public education on welfare rights so that the welfare rolls skyrocketed. They sat in at offices and schools, destroyed files used to police them, marched and picketed and generally obstructed the bureaucracy. They were visibly led by Black women, but their movement was thoroughly integrated (the majority of women on welfare are white) among poor women of Native American, Latin American, African and European descent. They drew substantially on men's power and their expertise in working the system. Throughout the 60s, they preoccupied the Kennedy, Johnson and Nixon administrations with their demands. And in the short term they won. The struggle continues today,[13] with the 70s and 80s Ford, Carter and Reagan backlash against workers, waged and unwaged, still focussed on controlling welfare, and with Black welfare mothers active in peace coalitions across the US, demanding the military budget.

As in the 60s, Black women winning on welfare is still central to the victory of the peace movement: it would be impossible for the American State to maintain its military presence at home and abroad without filling its ranks, now at least 30%, with the young Black men

26

and women who have no economic alternative to the US army. The US government is increasingly preoccupied with its army's lack of military will, which is said to show the inferiority of Black intelligence. On the contrary, the welfare mothers of these young people have educated them very well to get reparations from the US government for centuries of ripoff, while refusing the killing work. This is how one welfare mother made the connection between welfare and peace in 1972:

> If you think I'm gonna have a baby — and watch that child grow up with no food or clothing; and then watch him go to school where teachers don't teach him anything; and worry that he's gonna become a pimp or start shooting up dope; and finally, when he's raised, see him go into the army and get really shot up in there — if you think I'm gonna go through all that pain and suffering for an extra $50, or $100, or even $500 a month, why you must be crazy.[14]

# the black women's peace movement

*War is something very real to Belauans, not something we merely read about or see on television. We are also very aware of the health problems in the Marshalls — the highest rate of cancer and leukaemia in the world. I think this is what has made us the first nation in the world to have a specifically anti-nuclear constitution, which the US has not liked at all. They have forced us to vote on it several times over, but every time the people vote in favour — the initial mandate for it was 92 percent.*

27

*. . . there are US plans to turn us into a forward base for the Trident submarine and the Japanese want to dump nuclear waste in the Pacific. I guess that's how I became political . . .*

Bernadette Bedor, Republic of Belau[15]

*The nuclear industry, powerful, profit-oriented, totally unconcerned about our health, aided and abetted by a government that is its twin, is murdering us and our children every day. And it is up to us, each one of us, to stop it. . . . No time to quibble about survival being a 'white issue' . . . Massive demonstrations are vital. Massive civil disobedience . . . Talk with your family; organize your friends . . . Support those who go to jail . . . We must save Earth, and relieve those who would destroy it of the power to do so.*

Alice Walker, USA[16]

Speaking on behalf of a movement of Black and white women demanding back pay from the State for unwaged women's work inside the home and low-waged women's work outside the home, this Black welfare mother is saying that however poor she is, no amount of money can compensate for her son — the product of her work — being used as a soldier. She was speaking as one of the most ripped off people in the wealthiest country on earth, as a woman fighting for her money against the military's use of it in Vietnam.

Women's leadership in the anti-war movement of the 60s is visible today because women have taken organisational autonomy in the peace movement. By the same process, the organisational autonomy of the Black women's movement today makes it possible for Black women to claim the leadership that we have always given to the Black movement. And in my view, there has always been a Black women's peace movement — Black women have always been giving leadership to the peace movement as a whole by fighting on all the issues of Black women's survival internationally, issues which are still not recognised as 'peace issues'.

At the bottom of the international hierarchy of work and wealth, Black women have had to rely first and foremost on ourselves to insist that these issues be considered relevant to peace. That insistence has been our unique contribution to the rest of the women's peace movement and to the peace movement as a whole. There are not three separate peace movements. There is one peace movement of women, children and men, in which both Black and white women have had to take our organisational autonomy in order for the movement as a whole to come into its own − in order for the movement to move.

One contribution of Black and white women's leadership to the peace movement has been to show how private personal violence is of a piece with nuclear and military violence. There is a long tradition of making that connection. In Britain that connection was articulated by the feminist novelist and critic Virginia Woolf. It is one of the high points of my life to find in Virginia Woolf, a white middle class English woman − who in the 30s had to confront the fascism and Nazism abroad in Italy and Germany, while struggling with what she described as fascism and Nazism confronting women in homes, schools and offices in Britain − to find in Virginia Woolf what I know from my own experience as a Black welfare rights organiser in the United States.

For Virginia Woolf, the military was able to thrive because women did not have the economic power to speak out against them. Her response to the male-dominated anti-war movement was a call for 'a money wage for the unpaid worker' in the home. For both Black welfare mothers and Virginia Woolf, money in women's hands from the State was the key to the movement against war. And like Black welfare mothers, Virginia Woolf believed that the military budget prevented women from winning that money. [17]

These are twin points of reference for the women's

peace movement today. First there is the tradition of women in Britain fighting against all wars, including wars of Empire and colonial conquest. Then there is the tradition of Black welfare mothers fighting for peace from inside the belly of the monster, the US military-industrial complex. But our problems are not overcome simply by saying that the coming together of Black and white women would represent an unprecedented power. Reality is that it is not easy for Black and white women to see eye to eye, or even to know when we are seeing eye to eye, and to organise together.

# feminism, racism and careerism

*. . . to sell a brain is worse than to sell a body, for when the body seller has sold her momentary pleasure she takes good care that the matter shall end there. But when a brain seller has sold her brain, its anaemic, vicious and diseased progeny are let loose upon the world to infect and corrupt and sow the seeds of disease in others.*

Virginia Woolf[18]

*We always have a lot of programs – poverty programs, Model Cities programs – and they all are geared around the poor. But nothing is actually filtered down to the poor. There are a lot of jobs created for other people . . . We feel we're just urban prostitutes. Anybody can draw up a proposal . . . and say they are going to do something for the poor, and make a lot of money off us.*

Mrs. Johnnie Tillmon
Founding Chair of the National Welfare Rights Organization[19]

*. . . the professions have a certain undeniable effect upon the professors. They make the people who practise them possessive, jealous of any infringement of their rights, and highly combative if anyone dares dispute them. Are we not right then in thinking that if we enter the same professions we shall acquire the same qualities? And do not such qualities lead to war?*

Virginia Woolf[20]

There is a bad history that plagues us. There is the conventional racism: discrimination against Black women and preferential treatment for white women; white women accepting and imposing racist stereotypes of Black inferiority; Black women being forced to compete against white women for jobs, housing, wages and everything else — with Black women always bound to lose.

But this conventional racism underlies a still more dangerous racism by white women, more dangerous because it is in the feminist movement, which claims to speak for all women and to offer a better plan for the future. Let me give two key examples of this racism.

The first is over the issue of women having children. The movement's emphasis on abortion as 'a woman's right to choose' actually gave the State a convenient rhetoric and even at times a feminist ally, for perpetrating forced sterilisation of Third World women — both in our home countries as a condition of 'foreign aid' and 'development', as well as in metropolitan countries like Britain and the United States where Black and immigrant people are portrayed as a drain on the economy, and used by the system as the scapegoats for every social problem. Many white women who are considered feminists are active in promoting population control, while Black women are demanding the economic power to have the children we want, as well as the economic power not to have the children we don't want.

The second key example is careerism. The feminist movement has generated 'jobs for the girls' — as social workers, legal workers and lawyers, psychologists, sociologists, historians, educators, probation officers, immigration officers, policewomen, TV producers and journalists, government bureaucrats, politicians and prime ministers. White working class women share Black women's indignation that a movement built off the struggles of a great many more women than those who ever called themselves feminists, should produce women who are sometimes more efficient managers and exploiters of other women than the men they have replaced.

Both Virginia Woolf and Black welfare mothers highlighted precisely this issue of careerism as a major obstacle to the prevention of war. Virginia Woolf was preoccupied that women not do with education and the professions what men had done. Black welfare mothers were and are preoccupied by what they call 'poverty pimps', the professionals who make their careers by policing — monitoring, managing and planning — for the State against those they tell the movement they're serving.

On the one hand, women are poor and therefore need money, and on the other hand, when only a few get money they run the risk of becoming traitors. Both Virginia Woolf and Black welfare mothers agree that the way to deal with this contradiction is for women's unwaged work to be recognised with payment, so that women have economic power in their own hands to resist being compelled by individual men, employers, social managers and governments into supporting war and the economic system that makes war necessary.

In my experience what Virginia Woolf and Black welfare mothers have articulated is also the basis for Black and white women being able to organise together. I don't believe that we can win peace and all that peace involves unless we have the combined power of Black and white people, so that for me it is essential for the success of the peace movement that the Black and white women who are giving a lead should be pulling together rather than against each other.

When I spoke earlier about Black women's experience at the bottom setting the terms on which we work together with white women and with men, what I meant by terms was not the whims or prejudices of individual Black women who are not themselves accountable to Black women's struggle. Black women, as well as white women and Black and white men, must be answerable for the points of reference we choose: answerable for whether or not and how they reflect Black women's struggle at the bottom. Black women's experience setting the terms of our struggle for peace means that the direction and organisational priorities of the peace movement at any particular moment must guarantee that it not grow at the expense of those at the bottom. Otherwise the peace movement will grow, but it will accommodate war.

# pay women – not the military

*And is not the woman who has . . . to fight . . . secretly and without arms, in her office, fighting the Fascist or the Nazi as surely as those who fight him with arms in the limelight of publicity? . . . Should we not help her to crush him in our own country before we ask her to help us to crush him abroad?*

Virginia Woolf[21]

*Now hear me good. Poor people have a right to welfare. Poor people have a right to life, not just to look forward to death and life after death, or to look forward to somebody coming down out of the sky and giving you a beautiful life later. We have a right to live decently as dignified human beings today.*

*When I see money being wasted — sending men to the moon to play golf, dumping nerve gas in the ocean, burning potatoes, killing off hogs, mutilating them, just getting rid of them — and I see hungry and raggedy children running around, this is the kind of country that we live in, and this is what just burns me up. I feel the only way changes will be made especially in the welfare system, is through poor people, welfare people, organizing and raising a lot of hell . . . which is all we can do.*

Mrs. Mildred Calvert
Chair, Northside Welfare Rights Organization[22]

The common strategy of Virginia Woolf and Black welfare mothers which speaks to most women at the bottom is: pay women not the military. Such a strategy challenges all the economic power relations in the working class from the bottom up, beginning with those of us who have the least power, by placing the obligation to pay on the State, not on those who are only relatively better off than ourselves — the have-littles as compared to the have-nots. The strategy of pay women not the military places the responsibility for our economic exploitation on the military-industrial complex which has amassed our stolen work as their wealth. Pay women not the military is a strategy of reparations, and reparations for slavery has always been the strategy of the Black movement. Pay women not the military is therefore a strategy for peace that begins with the needs of Black women who are the poorest of the poor, while it includes the needs of all women.

A common strategy is essential to Black and white women coming together because it is the basis on which we can work together, each in our own interests, and on the basis of putting our own needs first, without white

34

women or Black women sacrificing anything, as women are always expected to do.

Pay women not the military is also a strategy against racism, in general and within the women's movement. Economic power for every woman in her own hands means Black women would be in a position to refuse to be dominated by white women, white men and Black men, and opens the possibility for white women to refuse racism, to refuse to degrade Black people as a form of compensation for the degradation of white people by the military-industrial complex.

It is crucial to building the movement that racism be defined not only in terms of attitudes. Institutional racism is about how racism is structured into and enforced by the economic and political institutions that govern us. Racism is essential to money-making and war-making, profit-making and world domination. The system rewards white people for being racist against Black people, just as it rewards men for being sexist against women, and just as it rewards some women, Black and white, for managing other women, Black and white.

Without striking at the economic roots of racism, we can't do away with racist attitudes. Dogooders may claim to be 'non-racist' or 'non-sexist', but we cannot base our lives on people who have more power than we do doing us a favour. At the same time, 'racism awareness courses' and 'sensitivity training' are making careers and money for a lot of individuals and a lot of institutions without altering the fundamental power relations of the military-industrial complex. The military-industrial complex profits from a race relations industry that indicts individuals for racism while it leaves the war machine intact — not only intact but even running more smoothly.

This perspective on racism is compatible with the tactic of non-violent direct action, which distinguishes between the person that one is confronting and the institution he or she represents; between the individual and the power structure, between the worker and the work; and which recognises, respects and supports – by organising collective action in order to build – the power of the individual to refuse to be used by the system against other people, to refuse to follow orders, to refuse to do one's job.

But non-violence can also be used to induce guilt and justify emotional blackmail. Already in the women's movement, Black and white working class women have felt silenced from expressing justifiable rage because of the touchy-feely ethic which dominates, requiring that you do not so much as raise your voice. By the same token, some men claim that the peace movement, unlike every other sector of society, is free of power relations between women and men because they have 'changed their attitudes' and are committed to non-violence.

# organising together

*A hierarchy of labour powers and scale of wages to correspond. Racism and sexism training us to acquire and develop certain capabilities at the expense of all others. Then these acquired capabilities are taken to be our nature and fix our function for life, and fix also the quality of our mutual relations. So planting cane or tea is not a job for white people and changing nappies is not a job for men and beating children is not violence. Race, sex, age, nation, each an indispensable element of the international division of labour. Our feminism bases itself on a hitherto invisible stratum of the hierarchy of labour powers – the housewife –*

*to which there corresponds no wage at all.*

Selma James[23]

*. . . we can best help you to prevent war not by repeating your words and following your methods but by finding new words and creating new methods. We can best help you to prevent war not by joining your society but by remaining outside your society but in cooperation with its aims. That aim is the same for us both.*

Virginia Woolf[24]

With the strategy of pay women not the military we can organise ways to fight racism in practice, and see our results not only in the objectives that we achieve – whether winning against deportation of a peace worker or a factory worker, or preventing the transport of nuclear waste through Harlesden and Cricklewood, in Brent, the London borough with the largest Black population in Britain – but also in terms of our process of working together across the barriers of sector; so that in the process of organising against the system, we are organising against the power relations between us that the system needs to keep running.

The subject of Black and white women organising together is limitless, requiring that we take inventory of all kinds of organisational possibilities. I have space for just two examples.

The first is about Women Against Rape which put government and industry on trial in Trafalgar Square in 1977 for rape and conspiracy to rape. The immediate occasion for the trial was that Queen's Guardsman Holdsworth was given a six month suspended sentence for sexual assault – so as not to interfere with his army career. In preparation for the trial, a contingent of WAR supporters invaded the Ministry of Defence, demanding the military budget on the grounds that it had never defended women, and that it was licence to rape and pillage all over the world.[25] Working together with Black

Women for Wages for Housework, WAR involved a whole rainbow of women in the trial, Black and white, lesbian and non-lesbian, immigrant and non-immigrant, mothers and non-mothers. Because the focus of the trial was indicting government, particularly the Ministry of Defence and the DHSS, and industry who 'uphold men's power over women in order to uphold their own power over everyone,' Jayaben Desai was as free to talk of her experience of rape by low pay at Grunwick as I was to talk of the rape of Africa by the British Empire that made my ancestors slaves in the United States, as other women were to talk about rape in marriage and on the street. If the trial had held only individual men responsible for rape, as some separatist feminists do, Black women could not have participated without condoning racist stereotypes of Black men as rapists. It would have been a racist trial, instead of what it was — common cause by all women against all forms of rape.

The second example is of the English Collective of Prostitutes. Recently the ECP badge, 'Whores Against Wars', broke new ground. Everyone knows that war and prostitution are inseparable — but the ECP has been organising to break the deadlock. In the speech giving his reasons for coming out against the Vietnam War, Martin Luther King described how prostitution was among the ravages inflicted by US intervention in Vietnam.

> So far we may have killed a million of them — mostly children. [The Vietnamese] wander into the towns and see thousands of the children homeless, without clothes, running in packs on the streets like animals. They see the children degraded by our soldiers as they beg for food. They see the children selling their sisters to our soldiers, soliciting for their mothers.[26]

The military-industrial complex tops up soldiers' pay with the services of prostitutes — that is, they compensate for the destruction of soldiers' lives with work that women, through our poverty, are forced to do. As in Vietnam, the plunder of the Third World and economic crisis in the metropolis make prostitution a survival option for Black women. And whether or not we actually work as prostitutes, part of the legacy of Empire and plantation slavery is that Black women are stereotyped as prostitutes.

The ECP's international network has been reclaiming and making public how prostitute women across the world have turned prostitution into a weapon of struggle and are challenging the military-industrial complex — from recovering the history of Black prostitute women in the United States who financed armed struggle against slavery which brought on the Civil War and abolition, to prostitutes in Southeast Asia who as urban guerrillas undermined the US invasion, to prostitutes in Australia who refused to service men from nuclear ships.

Campaigning for the abolition of all the laws against prostitutes — laws which criminalise women for resisting poverty — and for wages, student grants, benefits, housing and services so that no woman is forced into prostitution by lack of money, the ECP has been able to build a network of women from all levels of the sex industry. The ECP has been campaigning in all kinds of ways, from creating and developing a legal service for all women which rejects careerist legal workers and is accountable to the women, prostitute and non-prostitute alike, who use it, to the non-violent direct action of the church Occupation in London's King's Cross red-light area, where half the women working the streets were Black.[27] After the ECP sent a letter from the Occupation to Greenham saying 'if prostitutes had the military budget we wouldn't go into prostitution', some women arrived at the church from Greenham with their sleeping bags. As I look back on it now, I think the Occupation turned the church into a peace camp.

These examples show that with the strategy of pay women not the military Black and white women can organise together, each in our own interest, on issues as complex as rape and prostitution, which affect all women, but which have been used to divide us in the recent history of slavery and colonialism. In both examples what made it possible for us to come together was our focus on the State's enforcement of women's vulnerability. We were able to organise together on these issues because we made the connection between women's vulnerability and women's poverty – a connection which in each case led us to the military budget as a common demand.

The examples of WAR and the ECP also show that challenging government over the military budget is an immediate practical way of connecting apparently separate issues with the issue of peace, because all the issues women confront every day in one way or another involve cuts, shortages, lack of time and money, overwork, and a disparity of economic and social power between women and men in our most private as well as our most public lives. They show that the issue of peace can be made explicit in day-to-day organising on a variety of other issues, however diverse, difficult, divisive – disruptive of peace – they may appear. In other words, the peace connection is not an outside agitator.

The immediate usefulness of the pay women strategy is confirmed by the State's counterattack against the women's peace movement with the weapon of money: proposing that demonstrators pay for the cost of policing; confiscating hard-earned property essential to organising, like automobiles at Greenham; attacking our fundraising activities and the non-profit organisations we have worked so hard to build, through witch hunts, smears and cuts in government and private grants

40

to groups who refuse to toe the line.

Finally, pay women not the military has another immediate practical use: by recognising that it is first and foremost women in Third World countries who do two-thirds of the world's work, earn one-twentieth of world income, and own one-hundredth of world assets, it internationalises the peace movement as no male-dominated strategy can, connecting metropolitan women with Third World women, uniting immigrant women with the network we left behind in our home countries. Pay women starts with the Third World, acknowledging the fights that Third World women are making against what has been called the 25-hour work day; but at the same time it acknowledges that many of us have just arrived from the Third World; or though born here, still wear the Third World on our faces; or, whatever our colour, consider the inner cities and company towns where we live and work just more sophisticated forms of the favelas and plantations of the Third World. This is widening the issue of peace not as one issue in the service of other issues, or one sector at the disposal, or the expense, of other sectors; this is widening the issue of peace to encompass sex, race, class and nation all simultaneously.

# imagine

*. . . if your wife were paid for her work . . . a real wage, a money wage . . . your own slavery would be lightened. No longer need you go to the office at nine-thirty and stay there till six . . . You could see the fruit trees flower in spring. You could share the prime of life with your children. And after that prime was over*

*no longer need you be thrown from the machine on to the scrap heap without any life left or interests surviving ... in the care of some unfortunate slave. No longer would you be the Saturday caller, the albatross on the neck of society, the sympathy addict, the deflated work slave calling for replenishment; or, as Herr Hitler puts it, the hero requiring recreation, or, as Signor Mussolini puts it, the wounded warrior requiring female dependants to bandage his wounds ... the half-man might become whole. But since three hundred millions or so have to be spent upon the arm-bearers, such expenditure is obviously, to use a convenient word supplied by the politicians, 'impracticable' ...*

Virginia Woolf[28]

*What we want is a little money. You men know that you get as much again as women ... for what you do. When we get our rights, we shall not have to come to you for money, for then we shall have money enough of our own. You have been having our right so long, that you think, like a slaveholder, that you own us. I know that it is hard for one who has held the reins for so long to give up; it cuts like a knife. It will feel all better when it closes up again. When woman gets her rights man will be right. How beautiful that will be. Then it will be peace on earth and good will to men.*

Sojourner Truth, former slave, 1867[29]

Black women's experience — surviving, resisting, demanding, organising — at the bottom of the world hierarchy of work and wealth is a living critique challenging the many slogans so far put forward to connect peace with other issues and or to rally the peace movement to a 'wider cause': slogans such as 'jobs not bombs'; 'bread not bombs'; 'disarmament and development'; 'people before profits'; 'money for human needs'.

For one, there is no 'wider cause'. Widening the issue of peace must not mean subordinating or co-opting peace to a so-called 'wider' or 'general' struggle; nor must it mean one organisation or cause being used as a front for another, which is considered 'the real issue'.

42

Widening the issue of peace is a problem of how to organise: how to connect issues; how to connect situations and struggles; how different sectors of women, children and men can most usefully connect our different levels of power in a movement to which each of us is contributing, and acknowledged to be contributing, our own experience, issues and priorities, without undermining the least powerful. This cannot be done without taking account of Black and other Third World women, Black and Third World people; otherwise 'peace' is not wide enough to include most of the world.

For two, while each of these slogans rings true to some part of Black women's experience, the visible self-defined peace movement — which is dominated by white men — has so far had the monopoly on proposing and interpreting them on the basis of their experience and/or ideology, which is the experience and ideology of sectors of the working class who have more power, or have more power available to them, than most Black women, particularly in the Third World. Black women want more than the partial and temporary peace — or truce — that comes with connecting issues from the top down, on the terms of those who have more power, rather than from the bottom up, on the terms of those who have the least. These are terms of surrender, not peace.

For example, Black women's experience of waged and unwaged work; of how racism works in jobs; of the job market as a slave market: during slavery and since (who can call it freedom?) always being forced to work outside and inside the home (the slave quarters); always working the lowest paid and dirtiest jobs with the longest hours; always the last hired and the first fired in 'better' jobs; Black women's experience demands that we not settle for 'jobs not bombs' as the goal of the peace movement.

We have struggled, and are forced to continue to

struggle, for more and better jobs as access to more and better money; for jobs so as not to starve or die of boredom; for jobs as relative independence, relative power; for jobs as a major outlet which the military-industrial complex allows us for developing the talents within each and all of us which the military-industrial complex squanders; for jobs against governments which are determined to use unemployment, and the threat of unemployment, as a weapon to divide and destroy us. But no job has yet proved to be liberation.

I believe that most women, of whatever colour, are not convinced that the jobs men are forced to do are a bundle of joy and creativity either, that most men's jobs are emancipation rather than a meal ticket for themselves and their 'dependants'. Nor do we like having to pick up the pieces of what those jobs turn men into – picking up the pieces being unwaged 'women's work'. Isn't the peace movement about building the power to refuse 'men's jobs' – as soldiers, foremen, managers, police – both inside and outside the home?

And it is not enough to say that 'jobs not bombs' means jobs which are 'socially useful'. It is not possible to redefine what is socially useful work – work that we choose to do individually and collectively, for ourselves and each other – until we have access to the information and technology now dominated by the profit motive and almost exclusively at the disposal of the military-industrial complex; until we have access to the information and technology which are now making work and poverty hazardous to our health every day ('The Day Before'), killing us at our workplaces both inside and outside the home; until we have access to the information and technology which are now denied to us and lavished on arms and space war production, computerised surveillance, policing and social control; in other words, until we have access to social, political and economic power from the bottom up.

To give another example, the slogans 'bread not bombs' and 'disarmament and development', which aim to speak to how hunger and poverty in the Third World are connected to militarism in eastern and western Europe and the United States, can contribute to the continued imposition of 'development' and 'aid' on the terms set by the 'developed', that is, contribute to the continued ripoff of the South by the North, unless reference is made to the experience of Third World women. People in Third World countries are struggling to put forward their own terms for 'development', both to their national governments and to their international absentee landlords, one of whose strongholds is the World Bank: one recent example being the food riots in the Dominican Republic which challenged that government over its collaboration in implementing the conditions attached to International Monetary Fund loans. Elsewhere, Third World people have protested against population control as a condition attached to IMF loans for building schools, for example.

Robert McNamara's call for a declaration of 'no first use' of nuclear weapons by the United States, must not serve as a sop to the peace movement in order to hide his role as head of the World Bank. Third World women, who are now commonly acknowledged as suffering the most from 'development', are also the most experienced in being ripped off by the likes of McNamara, and by developmentalists – some of them in the peace movement. The peace movement can prove ourselves accountable to Third World women's experience by challenging McNamara's 'development' right in our own backyard.

The failure of the white feminist movement – with few exceptions – to make a stand against population control as a form of genocide against Third World people undermines the credibility of white women in the peace movement on the issue of 'development'. The military-industrial complex claims that population control is a solution to the problems of world hunger and 'development'. But Third World women's fight for the choice to have children who are not hungry, and the choice for mothers not to be hungry either, has forced even experts on 'development' to admit that the problem of world hunger is neither scarcity of food nor too many mouths to feed, but poverty — the scarcity of economic power.[30] In order to deserve the name, the 'peace movement' must be accountable to the terms of Third World women's fight for food.

Finally, Third World people wherever we live are increasingly refusing to aspire to the mess in the First and Second Worlds as the be all and end all of 'development.' We see the whole concept and politics of what is called 'development' as another form of racism, another form of business as usual for the military-industrial complex. We see 'development' as a kind of international race relations industry.

'People before profits' and 'money for human needs' quite simply fail to be specific to women — specific, that is, to the fact that women, particularly Black and other Third World women, are the most non-profit and needy, and the least powerful of 'the people', and are, therefore, together with children, most often seen and dealt with as less then 'human'. In order for all the people, and all the animals — human and not human — to be free, women must be.

For Virginia Woolf and Black welfare mothers, the strategy for winning peace was women's autonomy through women's economic power: reclaiming the wealth paid into the military budget by women's unwaged work — pay women not the military. According to Virginia Woolf, the 'daughters of educated men', whose poverty in their own right made marriage their only source of income (they moved from financial dependence on their fathers to financial dependence on their husbands), needed economic independence as the power to refuse to be dutiful wives who, on behalf of king and country, rallied husbands and prospective husbands to go off to war, and nursed the wounded and dying. In Woolf's view, these daughters were themselves so starved of self-expression and trapped by family life that some of them gloried in war as a refuge from domestic slavery and as an outlet for the talents which were repressed in the home.[31]

From another continent, race, generation and level of economic power, Black welfare mothers organised a mass movement which through direct action demanded money from the military budget and space programmes of the United States government. In demanding money against their own Black poverty in America, and protesting against their sons being used as cannon fodder in Vietnam, they were the backbone of the Black movement in the 60s and all its demands, and what those demands meant for Third World peoples and for the working class internationally.

To her credit, Virginia Woolf was quite clear that she could not speak for working class women. Also to her credit, she not only acknowledged that Black people existed (which many white writers still refuse to do), she referred to Black people's struggle in order to understand her own, acknowledging that her liberation as a woman was inseparable from the liberation of Black people, including Black women. For Virginia Woolf pay women not the military simultaneously expressed her opposition to sexism and to the racism of the British Empire and Nazi Germany.[32]

World War II, the Korean and Vietnam Wars, and several atom bombs later, Black welfare mothers — expressing their own needs in their own words, inventing their own tactics and making their own demands, in other words, autonomously — used the strategy of pay women not the military against the US Empire which had taken up where the other empires left off.

The situations of Virginia Woolf and Black welfare mothers were, to say the least, not the same. But their strategy was the same. And this seems to me an example of how from different vantage points pay women not the military can be common ground among different sectors of women; a common demand with which to find ways to work together and at the same time protect the autonomy of the least powerful; therefore a common strategy with which to find our way to peace.

Virginia Woolf and Black welfare mothers were demanding women's economic independence from the State, the military-industrial complex, as a way to survive and prevent war. They put forward a strategy for the peace movement which expressed their own needs, experiences and struggle — which the white male-dominated peace movement never said were about 'peace'. Pay women not the military demands changes in the power relations within the peace movement — between women and men, Black and white — as part of ending power relations, war, in the world. Pay women not the military says that peace begins with how we organise the peace movement — with respect for the autonomy of the least powerful, on the terms of their fight for peace. Pay women not the military says that in order to win peace the peace movement must be waged from the bottom up. Pay women not the military reminds everyone that we can't fight for peace without making reference to the people who are paying most for war: on an international level this means Black and other Third World women.

Virginia Woolf and Black welfare mothers challenged the totality of women's work, with all its expectations of what a woman is supposed to be. They rejected both unwaged housework and careerism outside the home. They called for economic power for *all* the women on whose behalf they spoke, so that women were not pitted against each other by careerism as the only alternative to domestic slavery. Both saw what careers turned women into. For both, the liberation of women did not mean changing places with men, or merely redistributing men's jobs among women.

By claiming back pay for the unwaged work that has already been done by the least powerful workers, pay women not the military demands reparations rather than jobs, more wages rather than more work. Pay women not the military puts paid to fighting over scarce jobs among different sectors of the working class, and demands the reappropriation of stolen wealth, information and technology rather than the perpetuation of drudgery.

Both Virginia Woolf and Black welfare mothers were painfully aware of how much men are coerced into State-defined manhood as breadwinners and warmongers by women's financial dependence on them; and aware also of the many ways men are penalised if they fail to measure up. They insisted that to free women is also to free men, who, despite how they are made to represent the military-industrial complex in relation to us, are nevertheless inseparable from us. They saw women's economic independence as the starting point for satisfying all human needs and giving power to all people. Pay women not the military can be the basis for finally leaving behind 'Victorian values' for men's sake as well as women's.

Pay women not the military is the grounding for those of us today who are determined to make the State, the military-industrial complex, pay on our terms for the war they have been waging against us with our money; who are determined to bring about peace by putting an end to the rape which forces women to do two-thirds of the world's work, earn one-twentieth of world income and own one-hundredth of world assets.

The road to peace, that hard row to hoe, lies through a minefield of power relations within the working class. Some men and women in the peace movement are

49

responding more or less violently to Black and white women taking our autonomy. But what Malcolm X said in 1964 still holds the promise of peace.

> You and I want to create an organisation that will give us so much power we can sit down and do as we please. Once we sit down and think as we please, speak as we please, and do as we please, we will show people what pleases us, and what pleases us won't always please them. So you've got to get some power before you can be yourself. Do you understand that? You've got to get some power before you can be yourself. Once you get power and you be yourself, why, you're gone, you've got it and gone. You create a new society and make some heaven right here on earth.[33]

Power to the sisters and therefore to the peace movement.

## Notes

1. Selma James, *Sex, Race and Class*, Falling Wall Press, Bristol, 1975, p.19.

2. On 12 December 1982, 30,000 women came to Greenham Common from all over Britain and other parts of the world, to 'embrace the base', linking arms around the nine-mile perimeter of the USAF (officially RAF) base, in the largest women's demonstration since the suffragettes.

3. Martin Luther King Jr., from a speech in New York City, 4 April 1967, a year to the day before he was assassinated; reprinted in *The Voice of Black America*, ed. Philip S. Foner, Simon & Schuster, New York, 1972, p.1051.

4. *The Guardian* on 13 February 1984, p.2, reported 'Home Office explains bar on East Europeans' who were denied visas to attend a peace conference in Scotland; and on 6 March 1984, p.6, 'Peace leader sent home': Dutch and French peace activists were deported from Czechoslovakia for attempting to meet with members of Charter 77.

5. 'Another dimension of the struggle in the schools was the struggle for Black Studies. I was very active in the 60s in that

fight, which involved not only transforming the curriculum but opening up the universities in the US to Black students, and all students, who didn't have the money to pay. The history of that fight is relevant to all the current attempts to change school curricula away from racism, sexism and militarism; it shows, for example, how implementing peace studies is inseparable from the fight against education cuts.' Wilmette Brown, 'Reclaiming the Third World Connection' in *Women for Life on Earth* magazine, Winter 1984, p.13.

6. See, for example, *The Voice*, 30 April 1983, p.7.

7. See, for example, *Peace News*, 21 January 1983.

8. Sojourner Truth, in a speech before the Equal Rights Association, New York City, 1867, quoted in *The Voice of Black America*, p.346.

9. *Women at Work*, International Labour Office Newsbulletin, No.1/1980, p.v.

10. 'Sus': the most notorious law used to harass Black communities in Britain, involving the arrest of 'suspicious persons' — most often Black youth, on suspicion of intention to commit a crime — on the word of the police. After a massive and prolonged campaign against it, 'sus', which derived from the 1824 Vagrancy Act, was repealed. But the same powers of stop and search are in the Police and Criminal Evidence Bill now before Parliament, and are already in effect in the enforcement of the prostitution laws, some of which derive from the same Vagrancy Act of 1824, and the kerb-crawling laws, which are used against women and men in inner-city red light areas (some of which happen to be in Black communities).

11. See Wilmette Brown, 'Roots: Black Ghetto Ecology', in *Reclaim the Earth*, ed. Leonie Caldecott & Stephanie Leland, Women's Press, London, 1983. In 1983 it was discovered (uncovered) that in Newark, New Jersey where I grew up, there was a factory in the centre of town where dioxin had been produced during the 60s for the Vietnam War. Like Vietnam, Newark is still contaminated.

12. Martin Luther King Jr., *Why We Can't Wait*, New American Library, Mentor Books, New York, 1964, p.137.

13. For an update on the welfare movement in the US today, see Margaret Prescod-Roberts, *Black Women: Bringing It All Back Home*, Falling Wall Press, Bristol, 1980. Available from King's Cross Women's Centre, 71 Tonbridge St., London WC1, 01-837-7509.

14. Mrs. Anne Henderson in Milwaukee County Welfare Rights Organization, *Welfare Mothers Speak Out: We Ain't Gonna*

*Shuffle Anymore*, W.W. Norton & Co. Inc., New York, 1972, p.83.

15. In 'The Land is Our Life: A Pacific Experience', in *Reclaim the Earth*, pp. 108-9.

16. Alice Walker, 'Nuclear Madness: What You Can Do', in *In Search of Our Mothers' Gardens*, Harcourt Brace Jovanovich, New York, 1983, pp.344-6.

17. Virginia Woolf, *Three Guineas*, Penguin Books, London, 1977, p.127.

18. Ibid., p.108.

19. Mrs. Johnnie Tillmon, in *Welfare Mothers Speak Out: We Ain't Gonna Shuffle Anymore*, pp.31 and 37.

20. Virginia Woolf, op. cit., p.77.

21. Ibid., p.62.

22. Mrs. Minnie Calvert, in *Welfare Mothers Speak Out: We Ain't Gonna Shuffle Anymore*, pp.29-30.

23. Selma James, op. cit., p.14.

24. Virginia Woolf, op. cit., p.164.

25. For the accounts closest to (though still not) reality, see: *Evening Standard*, Friday 9 July 1977, 'Mum-to-be injured in Ministry rape demo'; *The Sun*, Saturday 9 July 1977, 'Rape Demo Raid On Army HQ'; *The Times*, Saturday 9 July 1977; *The Guardian*, Saturday 9 July 1977.

26. Martin Luther King Jr., in the same speech referred to earlier, given on 4 April 1967, in *The Voice of America*, p.1054.

27. Legal Action for Women (LAW), King's Cross Women's Centre, 71 Tonbridge St., London WC1, 01-837-7509. LAW has been defending peace activists as well. For more information on the Occupation see *Network*, the newsletter of the English Collective of Prostitutes, and Selma James, 'Hookers in the House of the Lord', in *Feminist Action*, ed. Joy Holland, Battle Axe Books, London, 1983, pp.180-203.

28. Virginia Woolf, op. cit., pp.128-9.

29. Sojourner Truth, in the same speech quoted above, in *The Voice of Black America*, p.346.

30. Ann Crittenden, 'Poverty, Not Scarcity, Called Chief Cause of World Hunger', *The New York Times*, Monday 7 December 1981, p.1.

31. I think Virginia Woolf's analysis that some women rallied to war enthusiastically as an opportunity for self-expression can be extended to apply to a Black woman like Mary Seacole, the Jamaican doctress who served the British Army during the Crimean War. Though her situation was not the same as a white middle class English housewife's, as a 'coloured' woman Mrs.

Seacole certainly faced repression; and, in my view, the roots of her repression were the same – the British Empire, that earlier version of the military-industrial complex. She paid her own way to the Crimea and then set up her own business and nursing service because the War Office would not accept her as one of their nurses. As a Black woman Mary Seacole had to go to extraordinary lengths in order to prove herself and win recognition for her work, before the British Establishment finally judged her heroic. She tells her story in *Wonderful Adventures of Mrs. Seacole in Many Lands*, ed. Ziggi Alexander & Audrey Dewjee, Falling Wall Press, Bristol, 1984.

32. For example, see Virginia Woolf, op. cit., pp.61, 77 and 124, and Virginia Woolf, *A Room of One's Own*, Granada, London, 1977, pp.106-7.

33. Malcolm X, *By Any Means Necessary*, ed. George Breitman, Pathfinder Press, New York, 1970, p.64.

# Across the Divide of Race, Nation and Poverty *

I want to thank all of the women who were involved in organising this meeting for the time that you put in, as overworked as women are. I have some idea of what it took.

A lot of women have begun to write to me, or to speak to me when we meet in various places to tell me what they think about *Black Women and the Peace Movement*. It's really very important to me to know that what I'm saying is being heard and that women are finding it useful in their own situations, in their day-to-day struggles and organising. It's very encouraging for all of us who are concerned to build the peace movement, and to build all of the movements that are to transform this society and the world, to know that the kind of dialogue that *Black Women and the Peace Movement* was intended to generate is actually taking place, that those discussions between Black and white women, between Black and white men for that matter, and between women and men, are taking place in all kinds of ways.

I want to start by saying a bit about how I see myself as a Black American in Britain. There is a long history of the connection between Black people in the United States and Britain — not only our connection with

* Speech given by Wilmette Brown in Bristol, 28 January 1984.

55

Black people but with white people in Britain — that isn't brought to light enough. Recently in *The Guardian* some of you may have seen an article on Black American soldiers who were stationed in Britain during World War II,[1] and that is one example. My father was one of those soldiers.

Also, with regard to the history of the American military, there's a history of Black people's opposition to military service and conscription which the fact of Black soldiers having been here in Britain during World War II shouldn't hide. Some Black men refused to go into the American army in World War II because they saw that war as a racist war, a white government making war against a government of people of colour, the Japanese.[2] Many Black people, including those who fought in the US army, shared this view — which contradicts the official version of World War II as a war against German racism — based on our own experience of racism at the hands of the American State. Black people could not help but notice that Japanese immigrants and Japanese Americans were interned in US-style concentration camps while people of German descent, even Nazi sympathisers, were not.

It was announced just a couple of weeks ago that the British government was going to be applying directly to the US government for money to build some planes, Harrier jets. What immediately came to mind for me as a Black person with family in the United States, and knowing Black people are going through all kinds of hard times in America, was that the British government was going to get money in the name of British people from the American government in the name of American people to build planes: money which was going to mean that some more Black children would not have enough to eat, or that some more Black youth who are unemployed would be forced to go into the army. Which is yet another connection, because I know that the women who have been camped outside US military bases at Greenham and elsewhere have seen some of the Black soldiers who are here now as part of the American military occupation of Britain. Their presence is inseparable from the high Black unemployment in the US[3] which makes going into the army one of the best career options available. It's not a question of Black teenagers wanting to be in the army, so much as not wanting to starve, and wanting to have some bread, basically. So that while Black people are 10-15% of the US population, 30% of the American army is Black.

Those are contemporary connections. But there is, way back, another connection which is especially important for a meeting like this in Bristol.

I first came to Bristol in 1977, to speak at what turned out to be the first Black women-only public meeting in Bristol. There were rumours of threats from the National Front to break up the meeting, which was held at the Inkworks. Some white women came and stood guard outside the door of the meeting, defending Black women's right to meet autonomously; some Black men said they were available if the white women needed help. Some white women turned down our call for help because they didn't like what I stood for – and still stand for.

From the first time that I came to Bristol I have felt some sort of a connection going way back. I can't explain it scientifically; it's a feeling, a deep sense of familiarity with a place where I had never been before. The only way that I can explain it is to look at what the fact that I am a Black American has to do with Bristol. And that connection is the connection of the slave trade. I looked back on a little bit of British history, in a book called *Capitalism and Slavery*, a title which sums up a lot of British history, and found this quote:

It was the slave and sugar trades which made Bristol the

57

second city of England for the first three-quarters of the eighteenth century. 'There is not,' wrote a local annalist, 'a brick in the city but what is cemented with the blood of a slave. Sumptuous mansions, luxurious living, liveried menials, were the produce of the wealth made from the sufferings and groans of the slaves bought and sold by the Bristol merchants . . .'[4]

Now I doubt that most people here have lived in sumptuous mansions. And there is the tradition in Britain of white people who have participated in the Abolition Movement, and white working class people who starved rather than work on slave-produced cotton so that Black people in the United States could be free from slavery.[5] But as far as I'm concerned, particularly in Bristol, and for the occasion of this meeting, the history of the slave trade is the unfinished business of the peace movement. That is what we have to get to today in order to get more perspective on how women can organise for peace against the divide of race, nation and poverty. That is the legacy that we are dealing with, that is the legacy that we must overcome.

Now I've heard people say that Black Americans are obsessed with race, and in a sense we are, because for some Black Americans, slavery is as recent as our parents or grandparents. In this and other ways, it's a history that hasn't gone away, it remains fresh in our minds. I can't say that we know all the answers to the 'race question' by any means, but because we have had that experience, so graphically and so painfully, of living in a society so thoroughly divided by race, we have much experience of grappling with the problems of Black and white people organising together.

Some of that experience, by cutting through what race is about, that is, what it means to be divided along racial lines, makes it possible to understand power relations other than those based on race: power relations between women and men; between middle class people and working class people; and in general between people who come from different walks of life, however they may be divided and whatever the power relations are between them.

The solution to the problems of organising across the divide of race and nation and poverty — organising for peace — cannot be reduced to a series of gimmicks or techniques for 'racism awareness'. While the discussion about, as it's put, 'getting Black people involved in the peace movement' — itself a racist assumption that Black people are not already involved: whose yardstick is measuring involvement? — has focussed on some very practical steps that need to be taken, such as: translating leaflets into various non-English languages; considering carefully what should go on a leaflet or poster; going to the Black and immigrant press for publicity; holding events in Black and immigrant community centres; such steps by no means solve the problem of breaking down those divisions.

The problem of crossing the divide is obviously not unique to the peace movement. The same discussion is going on in relation to the unions, the women's movement, in local government, within the Labour Party, and so on. So that everywhere we're trying to deal with this issue. And often you get into a kind of double bind of some people saying 'Look, before we can have peace we've got to end racism.' And other people saying 'Well, we have to get rid of the nuclear threat before we can end racism.' For me, those two things are inseparable: racism is the bomb, which is already exploding and destroying millions of lives.

In building the peace movement, we are dealing with the unfinished business of the slave trade because it is the slave trade on which the military-industrial complex of today is founded. The point is that the divisions of race, nation and poverty among us are what keeps the military-industrial complex ticking. It is my concern to

59

make sure that there is no confusion between what the interests of Black People here or anywhere are, and what the governments of the world are up to; and no confusion either that on behalf of all the governed the interests of Black and other Third World people are the clearest and most comprehensive opposition to the plans of those governments. So that the problem is very fundamentally how we as women can cross the divide of race, nation and poverty in spite of what governments are doing, and as a way of withdrawing power and legitimacy from those governments, so that they are no longer able to carry on war against us or warmongering of any kind in our name.

Now before I get into more of how, practically, I think that can be done, I wanted to share with you a bit of a letter which I received on coming to the meeting. It says:

> I feel I should write to tell you, how for so long I, and no doubt many others, miss the *mass* participation of Black people in the peace movement. Having participated in anti-racist demos with my Black/Brown brothers and sisters, I felt their main preoccupation was with the discrimination against them, and that attitude understandable as it is, was rather narrow. I am pleased therefore to learn that there is a movement? Black women and the peace movement. I trust your meeting is well attended and may encourage the Black men to join the peace crusade.

It's from a man who is in Ex-Service CND.

Now, this is a women-only meeting. I feel it's important that it be a women-only meeting because we have barely begun as Black and white women to have the dialogue we need to be able to focus on how we organise together. But I also feel that a meeting like this has a responsibility to come up with some answers that men can also use to fight for peace and against racism. That is a responsibility of women's leadership. When we take our autonomy as women we have the responsibility of giving men that kind of direction, and it's in our own self-interest to do that. So I feel a certain kind of accountability to a man who lives in Bristol, whom I've never met, whose evaluation of Black people's participation is mistaken but who is nevertheless rooting for us as women to come up with something.

As a contribution to the debate which is raging fast and furious about racism and how to overcome it in Britain (and in the world), I want to give some examples of ways I think do not cross the divide, approaches and perspectives which aren't working, but which I've seen all about. I'm sure that you will have run up against some of these same ways which are supposed to be dealing with racism but which in fact don't. And when I say racism I'm also talking about nation and poverty: these divisions can't be compartmentalised. We're divided by colour, and according to our colour we tend to be ghettoised in different countries or different areas of the same country; and we have different amounts of money, different access to social wealth according to nation and race. Those power relations are all inseparable.

Let me give some examples of ways of dealing with racism, coming from both sides of the divide, that are part of the problem rather than part of the solution.

The Greater London Council has declared 1984 to be Anti-Racist Year. Now some people have said, 'How can you have a year against racism?' But I think that in itself is not a problem. It's important to focus on issues, and that's one thing a government or an institution like the GLC can do: it can try to focus public attention and put some of its resources and energy into backing those of us who are organising against racism. That can be a very positive move. But in the course of a branch of the State attempting something like that, all kinds of problems come up.

One of the slogans the GLC has been using is 'One

million Londoners are getting a raw deal because the other six million are letting it happen'. The effect of the approach behind that slogan is to let the State off the hook for institutional racism, that is, for racism that is structured into the entire economic, social, political, cultural and educational system which is imposed on everyone, Black and white. It implies that Black people are suffering because white people actually have the State power to prevent racism but are not using it because of their bad attitudes. It ignores and even hides the fact that the other six million Londoners are also getting a raw deal every day, and that racism is a problem that both Black and white people are suffering from, whether white people know it or not. In fact, from my point of view, white people's participation in the peace movement is already for some and should be for others a prime example of how white people can take responsibility for ending racism by organising against the military-industrial complex which runs on racism.

A Black viewpoint that I hear expressed quite often which reinforces that approach — that racism is a problem of attitudes, that you can divide the world in such a way that one million have one interest and six million have another interest and never the twain shall meet — is the approach of a Black woman who said at a discussion on health, 'Well, Black women's health problems have nothing to do with white women's health problems, and we can't really work together on the issue of health at all.' Now this is not to say that we don't have problems as Black and white women organising together — that's why this meeting was called, to address ourselves to those problems. But I think it is a mistake if we start from the point of view that we have no problems in common. Despite the particular problems we have as Black women, there are commonalities that are obvious. In the health movement there have been ways in which Black and white women have already been able to learn from each other, and build each other's power even to raise the issue of women's health, and to demand from government and the medical Establishment the quantity and quality of services we both need.

Another example, looking at the international dimension: it is quite a common view that white people in metropolitan countries like the US, Britain and the rest of Europe, are living off the fat of the land, living off the work of people in the Third World, and that the way to overcome this legacy of colonialism and imperialism is through self-sacrifice. People speak of giving things up as a way of bridging the international divide in standards of living. This perspective of self-sacrifice is a call to do penance in order to assuage the guilt of white people for the ripoff of the Third World.

Very often this self-sacrifice is expressed through changes in lifestyle, such as eating vegetarian, dressing from military surplus and charity shops, recycling and bicycling, trading in the underground economy and generally being less wasteful. While such changes are one way to withdraw our support from the dominant values and power relations, they are themselves dependent on the abundance, including even the castoffs, of the system, and by themselves do not justify the claim that they are compensating for the rape of the Third World.

Let us not forget that alternative lifestyles are also a response to our own poverty right here: for example, it's easier to live on the dole or supplementary benefit if you eat beans and wear secondhand clothes. But Black and other working class people organise differently against the same poverty: we may choose not to wear secondhand clothes — because that's what we've had to do all our lives, and instead demand higher wages and benefits wherever we can — without claiming to save the Third World. More and more people are realising that while not eating meat may contribute to improving health and bypassing the medical Establishment, it doesn't put any food in the mouths of Third World children. Insofar as alternative lifestyles are only changes in the style of our lives, rather than challenging the powers that be, they are actually accommodating them.

People of whatever race in metropolitan countries do owe something to people in the Third World: not only do the multitude of daily struggles for survival and liberation there confront the issues that are crucial for survival and liberation everywhere; those struggles give power to us here by challenging the military-industrial complex which rules us both.

But in paying our dues to the Third World, all of us who live in metropolitan countries must distinguish between guilt and responsibility: between, on the one hand, feeling guilty because our standard of living is higher and because the military-industrial complex which is based here is plundering the Third World in our names; and on the other, taking responsibility for opposing the status quo by using the economic, social and political power which that higher standard of living affords us to challenge and dismantle the military-industrial complex right where we live and have the most power to act. We pay our dues not by feeling guilty but by taking responsibility.

To assume that we in the metropolis have been living off the Third World is to assume that the military-industrial complex has not also been living off us. It is also to assume that the metropolis is all white — instead of including Black people who immigrated here from the Third World as long as 400 years ago or as recently as today, whether via the slave trade or as economic and political refugees.[6] It is a very white middle class point of view, a point of view of people who identify themselves and their interests with the metropolitan power structure, rather than with the struggle of Black and other working class people against the power structure. The perspective of self-sacrifice and guilt reduces participation in the peace and ecology movements to a disagreement within the military-industrial complex rather than a struggle to dismantle the war machine lock, stock and barrel. The perspective of self-sacrifice undermines the struggle of Black and other working class people in the metropolis because once again white people who have more than we do are telling us what we need and how to struggle — telling us we have enough — under the guise of helping us.

Another variation on this same theme contrasts the technology and wealth available in metropolitan countries with what is available in the Third World, and concludes that we in the richer countries can do with fewer consumer goods and much less technology in our lives. This can only be the viewpoint of people who have already been enjoying these things, who have had the more from which they can now consider scaling down to the less. Most people living in Third World countries, and plenty of people, Black and white, in inner city areas of metropolitan countries, have never had an automobile or a washing machine, let alone access to a whole array of technology which is available in the West, and they bloody well want access to it. They are not prepared to settle for less before they have even had a chance to have more. Again this is not simply a divide of race but also a class divide: most working class people, Black and white, are not into self-sacrifice — we already feel too deprived. I think the fundamental problem with this approach, sometimes spoken of in terms of 'appropriate technology', is that it can be a way to avoid challenging those who are controlling the wealth and controlling the technology. It says that people should take it on ourselves to scale down or give up, rather than wrench the resources, including technology, out of the hands of the powers who are monopolising them and depriving everyone of having them, in the form and the quantity which can enrich our lives without impoverishing our planet.[7]

It is totally unacceptable for white people or anyone else in metropolitan countries to say what is 'appropriate technology' for the Third World. And it is totally unacceptable for any sector of society anywhere to dictate what technology should be available to others. We are already suffering from such a technocracy, an elite which monopolises information, education and planning, and generally makes technology incomprehensible and inaccessible to the majority of people, particularly if we are women.

The issue is that Black and other Third World people, wherever we live (and I think white working class people as well), must have the power to determine what is appropriate for ourselves, and to determine our own lifestyles. And for this we need for white people who have more power than we do to concentrate their energies on putting pressure on the military-industrial complex to stop the rape and pillage of both the Third World and the inner city.

On the other side of that coin are those Black people who say that racism is only a white problem, that is, it is not built into the system but is an inherent part of being white, or that white people can get it together on their own, among themselves, to overcome it. This involves many assumptions: that because white people are benefitting from racism, it would be a sacrifice for them to give it up; that white people are not themselves damaged by racism; that it is not in white people's own interest to get rid of racism; that white people can overcome racism by an act of will — that any white person has the power to overcome racism; that since they have the power to give up racism — that is, it's not built into a system which they also have to mobilise the power to defeat — that they are guilty of not giving it up. All of these assumptions lead to encouraging guilt and self-sacrifice as a way white people can purge themselves of racism.

In my view, white people are benefitting from racism but they are also damaged by it. The system rewards them relative to Black people, so that it can rip them off. As Selma James says, 'Most white people are not privileged; we are just less underprivileged.' As I have tried to say, guilt and self-sacrifice can actually reinforce racism by letting white people off the hook: to challenge the military-industrial complex, they need only feel guilty and/or give things up. By this standard those who give up the most — who are those who have the most to give up — are the least racist, which means that Black and white working class people will never get together because white working class people have so little to give up.

White guilt and self-sacrifice also let those Black people who don't want to confront the military-industrial complex off the hook. They find it easier, more convenient, even sometimes more profitable, to be separatist: to hold white people *solely* responsible for a racist society rather than to challenge the power structure.

There is a world of difference between Black autonomy and Black separatism. Long and bitter experience of racism from white men and women, including those in the movement, has made it clear to Black people generally that we must organise independently. Very often when we take our autonomy in this way, we are accused of racism in reverse. But Black people organising without white people in self-defence cannot be equated with white people excluding Black people, which is a racist attack.

It is sometimes in self-defence against the charge that Black autonomy is Black racism that Black people say racism is white people's problem. I think racism is a problem that is imposed on all of us, which we must try to find our way through.

On our own behalf, it is important for Black people to distinguish between autonomy, which means organising independently in order to articulate our own case against the military-industrial complex as no one else can do for us; and separatism, which describes white people in and of themselves as the enemy. Autonomy – Black people defining our own interests and refusing to submit to racist power relations – can be the basis for Black and white people organising together, not in the first instance because we like each other but because we need each other to win. And on the basis of working together for common goals, friendship and love can develop. Black separatism fails to recognise that the military-industrial complex makes white people racist in the same way that it makes men rapists, and this separatism is self-defeating because it cancels out potential allies and thereby deprives us of the chance to win.

Another example of how racism works. Faced with our demands for access to power, the Establishment responds by trying to tokenise Black people. Tokenism involves the few Black people whom the movement succeeds in pushing into positions of relative power, being confined to giving the Establishment a new image, shielding it from Black pressure, and in many other ways enhancing its capacity to rule. The form of tokenism which is now current among sectors of the Establishment who consider themselves progressive (a term which means nothing to me) or left-wing, who consider themselves part of the movement, is to try to confine us to 'Black issues' or to the 'ethnic minorities considerations' of 'general issues'. So that it's not a question of Black people, in particular Black women, having something to say which transforms all issues in their entirety, and that every issue is in fact a Black issue; but that there's a separate Black compartment or Black dimension to issues, and a few Black people are allowed in to specialise in those. This kind of tokenism is an expression of the fear that a Black point of view on everything will go too far, challenge too much, and will be unmanageable even by progressives.

Another variation on the tokenism theme: some people claim that it's not important to get Black people into positions of power because that would only be tokenism, as though it doesn't make a difference if all the faces are white. The presence of even one Black face in a meeting room can transform the consciousness and decisions of the white people, at least till the end of the meeting.

In any case, it is not inevitable that tokenism will work.

In any number of situations, a borough council, political party, trade union or women's meeting, there has never been a Black person in a position to speak about his or her own situation, or the situation of other Black people. Black people harbour no illusions about bureaucracies, whether in the race or community relations industry, County Hall or wherever: politicking, backstabbing and co-optation constantly threaten to swallow people up, whatever their intentions, and Black people who allow themselves to be cut off from the grassroots movement outside are drawn, up to their eyes, into the intrigues and vendettas in the corridors of power. But at least if a few Black people are in there, Black communities have a foot in the door and hopefully – as we organise – can *make* Black people inside accountable. In other words, Black people outside can see to it that those inside use their positions to make some things known and get some things done. Black communities invest a lot in training and promoting people to go into institutions on our behalf. Here I do not mean investment in the very limited form of election campaigns. I am talking about a lifelong investment of mothers, neighbours, friends and community groups who teach, criticise, organise and demand every day, in the hope that our needs will be voiced and our issues pushed, rather than us being sold down the river again, by those of us who make it — those whom the community has made.

I come now to the women's movement and how some of the power relations between Black and white women are acted out there. A classic example of racism in the women's movement is how, with few exceptions,[8] white women's fight for abortion rights ignored and undermined Black women's fight against forced sterilisation. The State has been able to use the point of view of the most vocal white feminists — that abortion is 'a woman's right to choose' — as the rhetoric to justify the forced sterilisation of Black women.[9] So that feminists who do not recognise Black women's fight for the right — and for the economic power to exercise that right — to choose also to have children, supply the State with a 'progressive' facade to justify a family planning industry which has mushroomed throughout the world and which is often staffed by white feminist careerists, or at least by women from metropolitan countries who claim to have feminist backing.

Now that is an example of a division between Black and white women which is very obviously relevant to the issue of peace, because the whole discussion about family planning is bound up with the view that war comes about because of scarcity of food and other resources. The argument goes that if there are too many people, they are going to be at each other's throats because there's not enough to eat or there's not enough land or there's not enough whatever — therefore wars are inevitable and a war machine is necessary. Another variation on the theme is that 'have' nations need to defend themselves from the potentially invading hordes of 'have-nots'. That is how the family planning industry

70

feeds into the military-industrial complex, and is a vital part of it.

Population control is a crucial issue for Third World women, whether we are Bengali immigrants being injected with Depo Provera in London, welfare mothers or peasants being sterilised in Mississippi or Bolivia. Population control is a condition attached to Third World 'development' schemes through which 'aid' is doled out.

Starvation in the Third World when US agriculture alone could feed the entire world makes it plain that it is not the starving who are to blame for poverty because they have too many children, but those who decide on where the resources are to go and to whom. A growing Black and Third World women's movement, which has, among other things, helped to put into their proper perspective, the facts on the distribution of the world's wealth and resources and on the possibilities we are deprived of, seems finally to be cracking the walls of the family planning edifice, splitting some white feminists away from an industry that careerism and racism collaborated in building.

There are any number of examples of white women ignoring and undermining Black women, which has made it more difficult for Black women to acknowledge what we have in common with white women. One example of this is the denial by some Black women that the issue of women's right to determine and express our own sexuality has anything to do with Black women's liberation. The rhetoric to justify this position says that bread and butter issues are so pressing that the fight for sexual liberation is white and frivolous, a middle class luxury item, and not to be confused with politics.

Such a view further undermines Black women because a whole area of struggle in our lives, such as against rape and battering, and for the self-determination of lesbian women remains hidden. Therefore issues of vital importance to Black unity and to the liberation of all

71

Black people are left off the agenda of the Black movement, because Black women feel too defensive to articulate them.

Now to a more current example which shows how divisions between Black and white women are at the same time divisions between other sectors of women. Recent criticism that has developed in opposition to the leadership Greenham Common Women's Peace Camp has been giving to the peace movement and to the women's movement not only threatens to divide support for Greenham at a time when support is more needed than ever, but also attacks the very qualities which have made Greenham a breakthrough for the possibility of Black and white women organising together.

Greenham has been attacked on a number of counts. One of the criticisms is that Greenham reinforces stereotypes of what women's role is supposed to be; still another is that Greenham is getting all the publicity; still another is that Greenham is not based on any kind of theory, that it's just mindless activism without ideology.

That kind of criticism comes by and large from what I consider the old guard of the women's movement, the Establishment of the women's movement, which I'm glad to say has been upstaged. That old guard is responsible for many things which have not only made it difficult for Black and white women to organise together, but have reinforced the problems and the divisions that exist among different sets of women generally.

One of the key issues underlying the current debate about Greenham is the distinction between the strategy of separatism − which identifies the military-industrial complex as the tool of men, and the strategy of autonomy − which identifies men as the tool of the military-industrial complex. What I said earlier in the context of Black and white applies equally to women and men:

there is a world of difference between separatism and autonomy. If the military-industrial complex is the tool of men, we can bypass attacking the war machine and attack men instead. But if men are the tool of the military-industrial complex, if we organise independently of men, we can work out a relationship with them from that position of power in order to defeat a common enemy.

The strategy of the old guard of the women's movement, which has reinforced and created divisions between different sets of women, is epitomised in the criticism which scolds the Greenham women for not recognising that the problem is not Cruise missiles but 'the man next door'.[10]

This is a separatist strategy which is also racist — whatever the colour of the women putting it forward — because in effect it asks Black women to choose white women over 'the man next door': who may happen also to be Black; who may have proved over time, despite being a man, to be a more reliable supporter than any number of white women; and whom we may be dependent on to defend us against the police and/or the National Front. This strategy also demands of white working class women that they choose middle class women over working class men, again with little evidence from past history to justify that choice. This is to deprive the least powerful women of some of our protection and power against the State, including the power of our own local community organising with our neighbours next door and across the street. It is also another example of the feminist movement treating 'other' women, some of whom don't call ourselves feminists, as though we are too stupid to make judgements about which men are acting in our interest and which are not. It also ignores the fact that a cornerstone and major accomplishment of the women's peace movement has been precisely to acknowledge the connection between the violence of individual men towards women and the violence of the military-industrial complex; and to acknowledge that connection in practice by taking organisational autonomy from the male-dominated peace movement. And in ignoring, hiding — attacking — the victory of the women's peace movement in making that connection, separatist strategy also ignores the struggle that Black women like Esme Baker and Halimat Babamba,[11] for example, have made against rape, sexual assualt and battering by both police and individual men, in the course of defending the rights of the whole Black community. Separatist strategy demands that we choose between our right arm and our left, a choice that as Black women we refuse to make: as Black women we refuse to choose between white women and Black men, between being Black and being women.

I think that the old guard in the women's movement is coming out of a whole tradition of careerism, which sidesteps the issue of women fighting the State — for example, women having to deal with the police on a day-to-day basis — by saying that the problem is not the police but the man next door. The problem is not the State but the man next door. The problem is not the war machine but the man next door. If you want to become the State, which means being over other women and men too, which is what careerism is fundamentally about, then you have an axe to grind which is not for attacking those you hope will be your employers; then it is safer for you to attack the man next door than to attack Cruise missiles which, like the fence at Greenham, are State property.

I think that what is also at stake is whether, as different women who are struggling on a variety of issues, we're competing for the limelight, or whether what we're involved in is building a movement. There is a world of difference between using the media to build personal fame and fortune — another kind of careerism – and using the media against the media: that is, to spread the news and images of your struggle to more women than you could ever reach with a leaflet, and thereby strengthen their struggle as well, in spite of the smears and spying the media do on you while you're fighting to get them to cover your story.

One final example of ways of acting out the divisions of race, nation and poverty rather than breaking them down, is the discussion of non-violence versus violence. More often than not, this discussion goes on in code; it's not about non-violence at all. It's not about non-violence as a tactic or a perspective or a philosophy or a moral stance. Very often when white women, or white men for that matter, profess non-violence, it's a way of letting the State know that they don't intend to 'go too far', that except for a little civil disobedience now and again, they intend to play by the rules. (This has not prevented the government, with the help of the CIA and Nato, from treating CND as an army of subversives.[12]) And when they tell Black people to be non-violent, they are telling us to stay within the channels of protest that white people who have more power than we do have decided are appropriate.

So that non-violence is a code describing not only white people's relation to the State but white people's relation to us. Non-violence is a code for white people's fear of Black people expressing our anger, of rioting or whatever, and of having their own patch challenged by us. 'If these Black people are going to go on the rampage, if they're going to get violent, what they're going to do is come after me.' So that a non-violent position can really be about defending your patch, because what it does is to identify those who are 'non-violent' with protecting the same violent status quo that the peace movement should be about changing. Which I think is entirely different from non-violence as a tactic or as a perspective or as a moral commitment to change.

From the other side of the divide, there are Black people who dismiss the peace movement on the grounds that people who are into non-violence are not serious about winning. As I have said, claims to 'non-violence' may well mean that some people are not serious, and won't go the whole distance. But this view misses the point.

First of all, it gives the impression that non-violence is never used by grassroots Black people, when the fact is that Gandhi and Martin Luther King had followings of millions in the Third World, in the countryside and the inner city, who adhered to non-violence at least as a tactic for building and protecting the Black movement, if not as a philosophy. Many white people have been and are as seriously committed to non-violent revolution as Gandhi and King, for both of whom non-violence was not only a way of life but the only possible moral strategy for changing the world.

Furthermore, it hides that on a daily basis, even where Black people are involved in or committed to armed struggle, we are also using a variety of non-violent tactics. It's obvious that our struggles are too complex and too difficult to be limited to any one tactic.

In my experience we're involved in degrees of violence and non-violence all the time, to the point where it's very difficult, if not impossible, to distinguish between where non-violence ends and violence begins. Each successive movement develops new definitions of violence, and weighs up all possible tactics, in the course of building its forces and defining its aims.

So that the *real* discussion about violence and non-violence is much more complex and needs to go beyond this code which veils the antagonisms and tensions – the violence – which are the power relations between Black and white.

What we have to tackle, I think, is a refusal of work on all sides. Because it's very hard work to build a movement. It's very hard to make connections among people and among issues. Not merely links, not only an exchange of telephone numbers and addresses, but connections — connecting with those who have a different history and a different experience from your own on the basis of what your struggles have in common. It's hard work to break all the codes, codes which may make life seem easier while making it more difficult; codes through which we communicate while still entrenched in our divisions; codes which divide us from ourselves and each other. And breaking all the codes is what I think building a movement is fundamentally about.

Women who have experience in organising, whether peace has been their focus, or whatever has been their focus, know how exhausting it is to do painstaking organisational work from day to day, to take on that kind of responsibility: how to balance that with your housework, how to sort out the problems within the organisation, such as what kind of division of labour you should have, rivalry, power plays, laziness, carelessness, narrowmindedness, all of the antagonisms which develop, especially with scarcity of time and resources, and with the pressures and daily crises of the rest of your life. It is in sorting through all of those things that we connect, not only between each other as women but also we make connections between issues in such a way that, while we each focus on what we feel is the priority in our situation, we're not losing sight of all the connections, all of the places those priorities lead to. In following those connections, we avoid cutting ourselves off, isolating ourselves from other women in the process of isolating 'our' issues, 'our' struggle, from theirs. We gain access to the power of other women who are focussed on other priorities in other places, other women who can help us to win.

I've spoken in a general way about how racism, and

the divisions between Black and white women, manifest themselves. Racism pervades the whole of society and all our relationships. It can't be quarantined or surgically removed. Even when you are part of a network like the Wages for Housework Campaign which bases itself on bringing different sectors of women together (not only Black and white), every day you've got to work out how you're going to handle those power relations that day. I'll just give a few specific examples of the kinds of problems which keep cropping up.

One practical problem that comes up in organising day to day is deciding who's going to do what — the fact that there has to be some kind of division of labour. Who's going to do the errands? Who's going to do the clerical work? Who's going to do the planning? Who's going to chase people up to make sure that what's decided actually gets done? Who's going to clean up after meetings and make the cups of tea? This is a problem in any group, whatever the colour. But between Black and white women it is further complicated by the excess baggage of racial power relations, the extra work of ploughing through assumptions and prejudices about women's skills and capacities that are based on race. Sorting out, on the one hand, priorities among what needs to be done; what we actually can and want to do; and who is in the best position to do what at any given time, and how and when that needs to change; from, on the other hand, what we've been stereotyped as being capable of as Black or white women or what we've actually been trained to do, and limited to, by our 'station in life' — is an area of conflict between us that can flare up at any moment.

To give an example. I've noticed at a number of peace and ecology events that almost the only Black faces there are behind the food stalls. This may be the only way that occurs to peace and ecology groups to involve Black people in their events because they have no other contact; and it may occur to them as a way also of offering Black people a chance to make some money. But the picture this presents is blatantly stereotypical: almost every Black person present is preparing and serving food — which harks back to the slave plantation and the British Raj. Now it may be that Black organisations are not interested in participating in eco/peace events in any other way but selling food, and should certainly have that option made available. But as far as building the peace and ecology movements is concerned, this can't pass for making connections, and can justifiably be seen and felt as racism.

Then there's how to finance your activity. If you're building a grassroots organisation of any kind, chances are you start out without any funding. The whole idea of the Women's Committees of local government, the Greater London Council, Camden, Brent, and so on, giving grants to groups within the movement is a new thing. Women have had to start out by digging into our own pockets and paying some heavy dues to get an organisation going. So the question immediately arises: how do you work out what amounts of money people are going to put in? If there are differences in income between the Black and white women in the group — maybe there are Black women who are welfare mothers and white women who are social workers — how do you decide how much money each is going to put in? Or what if a white woman is on welfare and has decided to stay on welfare as a way to have the time and money to organise, and a Black woman is employed and bringing in a steady wage? What about taking into account women's childcare expenses — the power relations between mothers and non-mothers which may overlap with power relations between Black and white?

These are situations, which in my experience can't be avoided, in which power relations around work and money have to be faced on a daily basis. Now I have found that it's impossible to work through these daily power relations — that come from how we're slotted in as Black and white in the world — without having a common goal, without having decided that we have something to do together; and something in common which we use as a measure, as a yardstick, of where we have reached, and as a basis on which to work out how to criticise each other without being at each other's throats; as a focus for learning how to be sensitive and supportive to what each other's needs are and at the same time very clear about what we're jointly trying to accomplish. When Black and white women — or, in my experience any women — are working together, unless there is a clear sense that we are working not for each other but for a common purpose — common goals we've all agreed we want to achieve *for ourselves* — and therefore divide up the work according to how best to achieve that purpose, there's no way to cut through the racism of believing that certain types of people are only fit for certain types of work, and that a certain skin colour automatically translates into a certain income level. Common cause is also the ground for the honesty to face in ourselves and admit to each other the deprivations in skill that feel so painfully like failings in ourselves but which are the brands of our condition as slaves. Honesty which can be even harder to achieve because we have been divided and trained since before birth for the work of being women or men, Black or white.

Such a process comes also from appreciating that, however unaware of it we are at any particular time, there is always an exchange of power that is going on between different struggles that women are making. Once you've decided that the basis on which you're going to organise with other women, whether they are white women or Black women, is that you want to *do* something together, then you're not coming together first of all because you like each other personally; you're not coming together first of all because you sleep with each other; you're not coming together only because you live in the same neighbourhood, or because you socialise with each other, or because you come from the same background. When you look at socialising, sleeping together, who you're friends with, where you come from, and so on, these are the most obvious divisions among women of different races: we are separated precisely in those ways. By and large we don't socialise together, by and large we don't sleep with each other, by and large we don't live next door. So if we're going to talk about the basis on which we come together, it has to be on the basis of 'What is it that we're trying to accomplish? What do we want to do together?'

Once you begin to look at organising from the point of view of what are you trying to do — and that's what real organising is about — then you also begin to get a sense that much more is happening in the world which is going in the direction that you want to go in than you ever dreamed possible. You become aware that there is an exchange of power from other people's struggles — that you are being helped. So that when you begin to be aware of what other people are doing — whoever they are, whatever their colour and whatever they call themselves — you begin to be aware that there is more power for your cause than you knew you had.[13]

I want to give an example of that. One of the things that Greenham has helped to bring so massively and so publicly to the fore, much more than ever before really, is the connection between women and the police, and how women, in fighting for what is ours, in asserting ourselves, in challenging our status, are up against the State, up against the police. Now that's something that Black women have understood for generations. That's been our day-to-day reality. But the Greenham women, many or at least some of them have come from back-grounds where the police were not a threat. They didn't go out their front door every day with the idea that they might be hassled by the police, which is how Black people go out the front door. We never stop thinking about the police. You're out there in a Black skin and you think about the police, you know that you're in danger of being singled out for something, and it doesn't matter if you're Afro-American or West Indian or Asian or African, you have that Black face and you think about the police – it's second nature.

Now, what the Greenham women have done has led them to a position which is increasingly critical of police handling of women. Their own activity, what they themselves have done, that is what has led them to that point. Having led themselves to that point, the possibility of Black women identifying 'their' struggle with 'our' struggle is much greater.

That is an example of an exchange of power that is possible on the basis of what people are doing, what people are fighting for and against on a daily basis. But that has roots in something that went before. Again, bringing it home to Bristol, in the 1980 and 1981 rebellions in Bristol, Black people challenged police power in a way that in the recent period hadn't hap-pened anywhere in Britain. Whether it was acknow-ledged by peace activists or not, the fact that Black people challenged police power in that way put the police and police handling of every movement for change in the spotlight in a way that had not been true before, in a way that quiet organising over a long period of time had not been able to accomplish. So there was an exchange of power based on what people actually did: what Black people did (and white people who also participated in the rebellions) made a space for white people to do something as well. Despite the debate about violence versus non-violence, despite the fact that

Bristol rioters and Greenham women don't know each other and may not like or agree with each other about any number of things, despite the fact that the root can deny the tree and the tree the root, you can't separate Greenham from the riots that came before Greenham.

Now, to conclude. As I've said, I think that the Greenham women have been led by their own activity to a place where it's clear there's no turning back. Of course individuals can always turn back, can always cop out in one way or another. But it seems to me a lot of women have committed themselves for the long haul, for as long as it takes to dismantle the military-industrial complex. As a result of where their own activity has led them, they have begun to extend their connections and to take more responsibility for building a movement, that is to say, for making more and more connections with more and more people. That to me is the way to go, in terms of crossing the divide of race, nation and poverty.

Fundamentally it's not a question of whether you translate the leaflets or where you place the advertising for the meeting, but that you follow your own activity to its own conclusions and connections. They are no easy answers, no single cure-alls. No 'solution' to the problems of crossing the divide is a blueprint for success. The success of any tactic depends on how we use it and in what context, and on developing the judgment, based on experience, of when a tactic has outworn its usefulness. It has taken the movement a long and painful history to learn not only what is not at all guaranteed to work but also what is winnable in an apparently hopeless situation. Fundamentally what we have to get right for organising together is not only particular tactics, which cannot be reduced to mere gimmicks or techniques in 'racism awareness'. What we have to get right is the strategy: what we want as Black and white; who and what we think is standing in the way of our getting it; and who and what can help us to overcome that.

Now, my own individual connection with the self-defined peace movement (as distinct from all the struggles — including Black women's struggles — which are part of the movement for peace) began when I was active in the anti-Vietnam War movement in the 60s — and that and other organising in the Black movement and the women's movement in the 60s and 70s led me to the Wages for Housework Campaign. Our strategy has been to campaign for economic independence for the poorest and therefore the least powerful in order to: break down the divisions between women and men and between adults and children that are based on having different levels of economic power; break down the divisions between women that are based on having different levels of economic power — race, age, sexual preference, disability and so on; and break down these divisions on an international level where nationality defines different levels of economic power. We campaign to break down these divisions as we live them in our individual lives — each of us experiencing many divisions simultaneously, at war not only with others, but at war even within oursleves among the competing claims of our own multi-dimensional identity. Am I a woman, a Black person, an organiser, a vegetarian, a daughter, a lesbian woman, an Afro-American, an immigrant, a cancer survivor? I am all of these and more, and I will not be reduced by narrowminded sociological or political expediency to taking arms against any part of myself. My campaigning has led me to the point where I consider the breakdown of these divisions as one and the same as the breakdown — the dismantling — of the military-industrial complex, to the point where I consider everything that I am doing to be part of the peace movement.

So, by different routes, starting from different places,

I am led to the Greenham women by my own activity as a Black woman. The autonomy which I have taken in self-defence against the racism white women will inevitably express — including at Greenham — leads me, also in self-defence, to find ways of working together with them. My autonomy, which demands in me an awareness and acknowledgement of my own needs — like my need to call on the power of white women for my struggle — also demands of white women that they be aware of and acknowledge their need to call on the power of Black women for their struggle. I feel that as a Black woman in the Wages for Housework Campaign I am able to work together with white women from Greenham because of what each of us is doing: I feel we are able to cross that divide of race, nation and poverty — not overnight and not without hard work — because each of us, organising in our own ways, with our own priorities, is focussed on disarming and dismantling the military-industrial complex, and because in order to accomplish that we need each other.

Now, the connections between my Wages for Housework organising and organising for peace get even more specific. There are two examples. First, there was an article in *The Guardian* this morning called 'Moles on the Dole'[14] which traces the lives of three white women who finished university and are now unemployed. It shows how these women, far from being depressed and suicidal because they're on the dole, are having a ball. What they're doing is organising for peace. One of them is planning to go over to Northern Ireland where she wants to work on bringing Catholic and Protestant women together, as part of her peace organising, crossing a divide of race, nation and poverty. They are using the money and time which being on the dole makes available — time most women don't have in a nine-to-five job or as full-time housewives — in order to finance their work building the peace movement.

One of the charges against women at Greenham is that they are welfare scroungers. In fact, using welfare to fund organising has helped to build all the movements in Britain, not only the peace movement. It's a wonderful example — just like Black welfare mothers — of using the State against the State: using the welfare which the working class fought for and won from the State, but which the State tries to use as a weapon against us (keeping it low and degrading and full of hassles and policing), as a weapon for us to attack and dismantle the military-industrial complex.

The connection is that since 1973, taking our lead from Black welfare mothers in the US during the 60s, Wages for Housework have been campaigning against cuts and for increases in welfare, children's allowances, pensions and unemployment 'benefits'. We have been demanding that government payments be recognised as a wage which women are entitled to, without productivity deals and without means tests, including when we have a job outside the home in addition to housework. We have been demanding wages from the State, the military-industrial complex, both as reparations for centuries of unwaged housework and as the power to refuse all the ways that women are slotted into the system by our poverty. We have always considered this welfare organising as part of the peace movement because women have been able to use that money — and the struggle for that money — to challenge the right and the power of governments both to put women's and children's money into the military and to determine how women and children must spend our lives. So that my starting point, the connection I'm focussed on between welfare and the peace movement — these women are living that connection.

I was particularly struck by what one of them said. The article reports that 'Jane would like a career in the social services. "But failing that," she says, "I would take a job that was obviously for money, such as a check-out girl in a supermarket. I would never do something like a management course or a sales rep job or some other compromise career." ' And that really rang true to me. A lot of the prostitute women that I know feel that way about prostitution; better to sell your own sexual services than be put in the position of selling somebody else, or managing somebody else, as careers often force us to do, again reinforcing divisions among women. That's a practical connection, a practical exchange of power — I don't know these women, I don't know if they've even heard of the Wages for Housework Campaign, but there is an exchange of power and a connection between what they're doing and what we are doing. Women are crossing those divides, in their own lives, by their own activity.

So that the women's movement, or the peace movement, or any movements that we are simultaneously involved in, are not some kind of small closed shop of the 'committed', or only the ones who have the right-on theory, or only the ones who come to a particular demo. The movement is really much bigger than that particular part of it which is visible on demonstrations or which is visible at meetings or when the press give it publicity. The peace movement is women who are fighting for peace in all kinds of ways in their daily lives, in their own homes, just as the Black movement is that, just as the women's movement is that. And we can begin to *see* those day-to-day struggles, to break through their invisibility, and to see how they give power to these other more visible actions and focuses that some of us have come out to Greenham or come out to this meeting or come out to whatever to be part of. And we can begin to see that our numbers are much more powerful than we thought.

I want to close with another practical example, a way that people can, I think, organise to cross that divide of race, nation and poverty. Some of the Greenham women have started a campaign against Rio Tinto Zinc. RTZ is a multi national involved in uranium mining. None of the nuclear stuff can be made without uranium and RTZ is mining it — it's in the Third World, in Namibia, and among Third World people, Native People, in Australia and Canada. Black people, people of colour, are dying now of disease because the stuff is so polluting to those who are taking it out of the ground and to those who live near where it's being mined. That means we are already suffering nuclear devastation *before* The Day After.

The Greenham initiative is able to build on the work of many other women and men who have been organising in Britain against RTZ. They are also building on and getting power from Black people's struggle for liberation in southern Africa.

So Greenham women have begun this initiative of calling everyone's attention to what RTZ is doing. They have prepared a list of the local councils throughout Britain that have shares in Rio Tinto Zinc, and three and a half million of those shares belong to local councils which have declared themselves nuclear-free zones. So there's practical organising that can be done in a lot of different places about that. When you look at the women who are affected by RTZ and the women who are opposing RTZ in various ways, you see that we cross all kinds of national boundaries, all kinds of boundaries of income and of race. This initiative by some Greenham women is one which speaks to the situation of Black women, something which Black women can connect with. (I'm very impressed; at the end of this Greenham leaflet about RTZ, as a signing off, it says 'January 1984. Dear Queen Elizabeth. Asking you to take note of the fact that a lot of your money is invested in Rio Tinto Zinc.')

From the slave trade, to the military-industrial

complex, one stronghold of which is Rio Tinto Zinc. The unfinished business of the peace movement.

Unfortunately, we've had some failures. We've had a lot of blows in the past, and there are more blows to come. A woman like Virginia Woolf, who inspires me so much and encourages me to believe that I'm on the right track in terms of how to bridge those gaps, make those connections, cross those divides between women, a woman like Virginia Woolf committed suicide. The movement did not yet have the power to keep her alive.

We have no excuse. We have the power not to commit suicide, in the many ways that we do it, one of those ways being to stay in our little ghettoes and not dare to cross those divides. We have the power now to cross the divide of race, nation and poverty, and we have no excuse for not doing it. Because together we can win.

## Notes

1. 'How racism came to Britain with the American Army' by Lotte Hughes, *The Guardian*, 7 January 1984, p.6.

2. We cannot forget that Black Americans were not the only ones to see the war against Japan that way. Many Indians, in the cause of national liberation, joined with the Japanese on the basis of their common war against the racist British.

3. 'Formula Links Economy, Recruiting', Tom Philpott, *Army Times*, 4 October 1982.

Between July 1973, and September 1981, 42 percent of all black males between the ages of 18 and 23 who were qualified for military service joined the Army, Navy, Air Force or Marine Corps. In contrast, during this period only 14 percent of the qualified white males and 15 percent of the qualified Hispanic males enlisted . . . the percentage of qualified blacks who joined the military during the period actually may be as high as 50 percent.' '42% of Eligible Blacks Enlist in the Services', Tom Philpott, *Army Times*, 7 June 1982.

'High unemployment has been a major factor in increased military enlistment, says Dr. Martin Binkin, a defense specialist with the Brookings Institution . . . The Military has been the

principal employer of young blacks [*sic*: i.e. Black men] . . .'
'Military Faces Dilemma as enlistment of jobless grows', *Christian Science Monitor*, 19 November 1982.

'New education benefits, pay hikes, and cash bonuses are just a few of the carrots the military danglès in front of potential recruits. One Army assistance program provides as much as $15,000 in educational funds after only a two-year tour of duty.

'. . . "The Army is now viewed as a means to an end," says one recruiter in the Pittsburgh area. "Just look at our ad campaign – 'Be all you can be.'"

'. . . "The big reason people join up is job training," says [a recruiter] . . . near Chicago.' 'Army's new recruiter: recession', *Christian Science Monitor*, 4 February 1982.

This information was obtained from the *Poverty Draft Packet*, an excellent file put together by Project STP (Stop the Pentagon/Serve the People), PO Box 13416, Philadelphia PA 19101, (215) 296-4875. Project STP offers help to GIs and to people facing both the draft and enlistment – 'the poverty draft'.

4. Eric Williams, *Capitalism and Slavery*, André Deutsch, London, 1964, p.61.

5. See, for example, Karl Marx's report on 'A London Workers' Meeting', published in *Die Presse*, 2 February 1862; reprinted in English in Karl Marx & Frederick Engels, *On Britain*, Moscow, 1953, pp.459-63. It seems to me that no discussion of racism in Britain can afford to ignore this outstanding example of international solidarity between white wage slaves and Black chattel slaves.

6. 'In 1981 people from Haiti who had immigrated to the US were told by the US government that they couldn't stay there because they weren't refugees; and they said, 'Oh yes, we're all refugees, we're economic refugees.' And when they said that, they were really speaking for all immigrant women and for all immigrant people, because that's what we all are . . .' Nina Lopez-Jones in *Strangers and Sisters: Proceedings of a women's conference on race and immigration*, ed. Selma James, Falling Wall Press, Bristol, 1984.

7. We are often asked to choose between the environment on the one hand and technology on the other. It is absurd to assume that these are inevitably opposed. The enemy is the aims and purposes of those who control the research, design, production, costing and distribution of the present technology. To direct our energy against technology *per se* is to miss the point and even strengthen the political hand which controls the electronic

robot that now chokes us.

8. The International Wages for Housework Campaign and the Feminist Women's Health Center are the exceptions I know about. The Campaign has always said that if you cannot afford to have children (or more children), that is a form of sterilisation, and that financial independence is the power to have or not to have children. Unlike many career women in the feminist movement, grassroots Black and white women did not lose sight of the connection between money and control over our own bodies. The Feminist Women's Health Center has often been attacked in the women's movement for refusing to go along unconditionally with the pro-abortion movement, and has taken responsibility for attending international conferences of doctors on birth control, when it could ill afford the fares, in order to disrupt CIA-planned parenthood (i.e. sterilisation). Their attitude has always been that this is their responsibility as metropolitan women to Third World women.

My confidence in women makes me believe there must be other organisational examples. It is also important to remember that not only women of colour suffer forced sterilisation by the American State. Many poor white women are also sterilised.

9. In the March/April 1984 issue of *New Directions for Women*, an American feminist bi-monthly, is a photo of a women's demonstration in Washington DC in 1981. In it a woman is carrying a placard saying, 'Abortion: a Woman's Right to Choose'. Since then *New Directions* (?) have published several letters from 'feminists' defending US government population control policies in the Third World as being what they consider to be in the interests of Third World women. In *Science* magazine as far back as 27 February 1970, an article by Luther J. Carter made clear that '. . . the recent growth of the feminist movement . . . makes it a force to be reckoned with. The first to discover this may be those government officials and members of Congress who seek to lower the birth rate.' (p.1236) It is significant that feminists in the 80s still seem largely oblivious to the sterilisation side of the reproductive rights issue — just as Congress would have wanted them to be.

10. 'Is Greenham Feminist?', in *Breaching the Peace*, Onlywomen Press, London, 1983, pp.20-1.

11. In 1982 (see *The Guardian*, 26 October 1982) Esme Baker won her campaign against the Walthamstow (London) police: she was cleared of police charges against her for assaulting them — which was their cover for her charge that they had sexually assualted her. In 1983 Halimat Babamba won her campaign

91

against being deported after she had left her violent husband — deportation itself being a form of State violence against Black people. Halimat had been dependent on her husband's visa for permission to stay in Britain. Women Against Rape and Black Women for Wages for Housework campaigned steadily in support of these courageous sisters. Esme's solicitor, Paul Boateng, told us outside the courtroom on the day Esme won her case that she couldn't have won without us filling the courtroom and picketing outside during the trial. For more information, contact King's Cross Women's Centre, 71 Tonbridge St., London WC1, 01-837-7509.

12. See 'The curse of the President's men', Susan Thomas, *The Guardian*, Saturday 8 October 1983, p.7.

13. One recent important example of this is how picketing during the miners' strike helped to keep police so busy they had to delay evicting Greenham women from the Main Gate for lack of sufficient 'troops'.

14. *The Guardian*, Saturday 28 January 1984.

# THE RAPIST WHO PAYS THE RENT

## Women's Case for Changing the Law on Rape

### by Ruth Hall, Selma James & Judit Kertesz

The handbook of the movement to make rape in marriage a crime, up to date with new developments in Britain and abroad. Covering also rape by strangers, the rape of children, and rape in court, this book shows how the rape laws actually work. With a Foreword by Wilmette Brown, 'From Private Pain to Public Protest: Rape and Race'.

Paperback   68 pages   ISBN 0 905046 27 7   £2.25

*New Edition June 1984*

 **FALLING WALL PRESS**

*For a complete list
of Falling Wall Press publications
please write to
75 West Street
Old Market
Bristol BS2 0BX
England*